THE SIX
CONVERSATIONS
OF A BRILLIANT
MANAGER

PRAISE FOR *THE SIX CONVERSATIONS OF A BRILLIANT MANAGER*

'Every manager could learn something of real value from this book'

Carrie Bedingfield, Founder, Onefish Twofish

'I recommend this book to new and existing managers who want to be successful and brilliant in their role'

Dr Abi Layton, Research Scientist

'*The Six Conversations of a Brilliant Manager* is quite simply a brilliant book'

Anthony Sheldon, Master Executive Coach and Managing Director, Mudita Coaching Ltd

THE SIX CONVERSATIONS OF A BRILLIANT MANAGER

A BUSINESS STORY FOR MANAGERS
(and anyone who has a manager)

ALAN J. SEARS

Red Door

Published by RedDoor
www.reddoorpublishing.com

© 2019 Alan J. Sears

The right of Alan J. Sears to be identified as author of this Work has been asserted by him in accordance with sections 77 and 78 of the Copyright, Designs and Patents Act 1988

All rights reserved. No part of this publication may be reproduced, stored in a retrieval system, copied in any form or by any means or otherwise transmitted without written permission from the author

A CIP catalogue record for this book is available from the British Library

Cover design: Rawshock Design

Typesetting: Tutis Innovative E-Solutions Pte. Ltd

CONTENTS

Part I: The Story
1. Lucky for Some 3
2. Meet the Team 6
3. Dilemma 11
4. Home Truths 12
5. Sage Advice 14
6. Tom, Huck and Mark 18
7. Coaching (Conversation #1: 'What can you do about that?') .. 20
8. Accountability (Conversation #2: 'Who should really own this?') .. 26
9. More Than One Way 33
10. Blue Monday 37
11. In It Together 40
12. Kudos 43
13. Busy Busy (Conversation #3: 'How should we be behaving?') .. 47
14. Teenage Kicks 51
15. Delegation (Conversation #4: 'Who's really doing this?') .. 56
16. Hearts and Minds 64
17. Curfew 66
18. Career (Conversation #5: 'Where are we heading?') .. 68
19. Preparation 75
20. Appraisal (Conversation #6: 'How are we doing?') .. 77
21. Consideration 84
22. Short Weekend 89

23.	Practice	93
24.	Celebration-Karaoke	97
25.	Dragon's Den	99
26.	Tell Me More	106
27.	One Month Later	109

Part II: The Conversations

1.	Conversation #1: 'What can you do about that?'	113
2.	Conversation #2: 'Who should really own this?'	114
3.	Conversation #3: 'How should we be behaving?'	116
4.	Conversation #4: 'Who's really doing this?'	117
5.	Conversation #5: 'Where are we heading?'	119
6.	Conversation #6: 'How are we doing?'	121

Acknowledgements	127
About the Author	135

PART I: THE STORY

CHAPTER 1

LUCKY FOR SOME

Sam Mitchell had never really believed in luck. That was until the day he was told he was UK Operations Manager for the exciting start-up he had joined only a few months before. After all, when your boss leaves to follow her boss off to a new opportunity it is easy to see that as a door opening for you.

DecisionMaker.com had just moved to Hoxton, London's sexy new home for all kinds of tech businesses. Sam didn't quite fit the hipster mould that seemed to be all the rage, but he had been doing his best. After all, being good at what you do and producing the right results had to count for more than the way you looked and having the right kind of beard, right? As it happened, Sam's wife preferred him clean-shaven, as did his daughter, Emma, and given the challenges her teenage years were providing, Sam was very keen to promote harmony at home as well as at work.

In truth, Sam had some misgivings when Dr Kramer had made him the offer. To be more accurate, it hadn't really been an offer. Kramer had simply said: 'I want you to be Operations Manager, Sam. We are recruiting for a new Operations Director but that may take some time. So for now you'll be in charge. Don't let me down.'

Arnold Kramer was undoubtedly clever. He had a PhD and was the intellectual founder of DecisionMaker. The product was based on his research into why people often make bad decisions, and what to do about that. He was also ambitious for more than academic success. His research paper had been followed by a popular book that had sold well, though it had to be ghostwritten because Arnold did not exactly have the popular touch in his prose. He could not quite escape the need to show off his brilliance and encyclopaedic knowledge on every page. Nor could he shake off the idea of his academic colleagues sniffing at every page and pointing out a lamentable lack of rigour.

A tech writer called Don Hale had solved both of those problems whilst vowing that he would never work with Kramer again. 'Every conversation with him is just another excuse for an argument,' was all he would say when asked. Before parting company, Hale had told Kramer that the book should have a website with the usual set of tools and resources, a blog, links to other useful sites and so on. Whilst initially sceptical about the idea, Kramer rapidly became an enthusiast. He could see how his research could be turned into an intelligent problem-solving tool. Ask it a question and it wouldn't tell you what decision to make, but it would coach you to making a well-thought-out decision and avoid some of the more common decision-making biases. Arnold Kramer's real genius, however, lay not in seeing the commercial possibilities of the idea, but in finding Dale Howson.

Howson was a genius in his own right. He was an expert in systems that use a natural language user interface to answer questions, make recommendations, and in particular, ask questions of the user and process the answers. His previous company had been bought up by a global giant and in spite of all offers and entreaties to stay, the culture shift hadn't worked for him. Meeting Arnold Kramer at a networking event had seemed like a godsend, and DecisionMaker.com was born.

With no shortage of venture capital behind the start-up, and engineers queuing up to join, DecisionMaker grew rapidly. Then things started to get sticky. Deadlines were missed. Solution-finding became replaced by finger-pointing. The culture that had kept everyone glued together – and glued to their work – appeared to be coming apart. Dale Howson seemed to become more and more involved in technical issues, neither very available nor very visible, while Arnold Kramer seemed to be everywhere, pointing his finger, stirring resentment and generally being unhelpful. His unwitting catchphrase, 'What you need to do is …' became widely mimicked behind his back.

Sam had not really been aware of any of this. He had kept his head down, tried to avoid people who were becoming negative and cynical, and got on with things. That his boss had followed her boss out of the door hadn't been that big a shock as the two of them had worked together before. Sam figured one of them had spotted the next new-new thing, or so they thought, had shared the news, and they had both jumped ship together. As it turned out, what seemed like a stroke of luck was very nearly Sam's undoing.

CHAPTER 2

MEET THE TEAM

Arnold Kramer told the team, who seemed slightly surprised but said nothing. If anyone else thought they should have got the job they certainly weren't showing it. Sam scanned the body language in the meeting room and drew a blank. There were a couple of murmurs of 'well done' and that was about it. Sam had prepared a few words, nothing much, just that it was a great team, he was proud to be Ops Manager, he wasn't about to make any major changes – oh, and he knew everyone had a lot to do so 'let's all get back to it.' He got a nod from Arnold Kramer.

Sam went back to his station and stared at his screen, where the mission for Operations stared back at him. His former boss, Kathy, rather than the departed director, had defined the mission for Operations: 'Driving operational excellence across the organisation.'

Sam pulled a lined notebook and a roller-ball pen out of his satchel.

At the top of a clean page he wrote 'What are we really here for?' in block letters, and then set about answering his own question. He thought about allocating resources, managing freelancers, engaging partners, defining policies and processes, and a dozen other things until his head swam. Finally he wrote down 'We are here to make this business work better.'

He glanced back up at his screen. Underneath the mission directive there was another reminder.

'We are here to challenge everything. As the masters of efficiency, we are constantly looking for better ways to get things done.'

Sam thought about money and budgets. The Operations team worked with Finance to develop budgets and then manage operations to meet the budget goals. Revenue forecasts belonged with Sales and the monthly profit and loss figures with Finance, but Sam's new role would include reviewing profitability across the business and taking action as needed.

What, he wondered, would Kathy see as the priority if she were still here? One of Kathy's major preoccupations had been resourcing. 'Do we have the right people in place?' Sam wondered. He wasn't at all sure that there was a sufficiently talented pool of freelancers in place to pull from as needed, and he had very little idea how staff were assigned to projects. Kathy had spent a lot of time with HR – something Sam would have to get used to.

A notification flicked up on his screen but his eye was caught instead by Kathy's next statement: 'We challenge the basic assumptions underlying each department's operations.' Right now the only thing Sam felt like challenging was his own competence to do the job he had just been given.

He was saved from an unhelpful descent into self-pity by the arrival of Rosie Channing. Rosie was DecisionMaker's Workplace Evangelist. Elsewhere she would probably have been called something like Facilities Coordinator but everyone at DecisionMaker got to choose their own job title. Arnold Kramer had been vigorously opposed to this idea. He thought it silly, flippant, irrelevant, unhelpful, and a number of other things, but for once Dale's view had prevailed and so Rosie was a Workplace Evangelist.

Rosie was responsible for the office design, the layout of furniture and other equipment, and how that affected the efficiency and profitability of DecisionMaker. As well as buying office furniture and supplies, Rosie's role included determining when more space was needed, choosing appropriate suppliers, and managing the facilities budget. Her real passion, however, was creating a great workplace. Somewhere people would want to come into. Rosie's goal was to make DecisionMaker everyone's favourite place to be.

Rosie had the right personality to be an evangelist: she was bright, bouncy, energetic and full of ideas. Sam had noticed, however, that a lot of Rosie's energy went into things that didn't seem to have much impact or make much difference, and many of her ideas never got any further than just being a good idea. Privately, he had his own theory about why that was. While he liked Rosie's energy and enthusiasm, he could see that such intensity could almost be a turn-off for Dale and Arnold. They liked things presented in a cooler, calmer fashion, backed up by information and data. If Rosie was going to be truly effective in her role then she was going to need help.

As usual Rosie burst into his station, almost breathless with excitement.

'Sam, I think it's brilliant that you are Ops Manager! There is so much I want to do, and I always felt that Kathy, although I really liked her, was continually putting the brakes on things. I have so many great ideas about how we can make this the best office space in London – in terms of how people feel about being here, I mean, and I just know I can get so much done with you supporting me!'

'Well I'm really pleased you feel that way, Rosie,' Sam began cautiously. 'Of course, I'm going to need a few days to look at everything before we start making any big decisions.' He could see Rosie's big smile begin to fade and dug deep for a way to rescue the conversation without having to listen to a whole raft of Rosie's latest ideas, or, even worse, agreeing to action some of them before he'd had time to consider things properly. He managed a big grin of his own. 'The thing is, Rosie, I am going to have to put forward an integrated plan for Operations, so I need to talk to everyone and make sure that anything you and I want to do doesn't interfere with anything else that is going on in another part of the business. How about you put together a list of the top ten things you think would have most impact? Make sure there are a couple of quick wins in there and some things that won't cost too much. Get that back to me, then we can sit down and look at what the best way forward would be.'

Rosie revived a bit, and agreed fairly cheerfully. Sam breathed a quiet sigh of relief, whilst inwardly acknowledging that all he had really done was buy some time. Although he did give himself some credit for limiting Rosie to ten things. It still wouldn't be an easy conversation, but ten things they could take one at a time would be a lot better than Rosie firing off every idea in her head all at once.

Sam flicked up his team Org Chart on to the screen. It looked something like a mind-map with the roles arranged in a circle, each containing the employee's name, their chosen job title, and a brief explanation of what that job entailed. Working clockwise from Rosie, next came Sayeed, DecisionMaker's Getter of Great Stuff, or Procurement Analyst for the more prosaically minded.

Sam knew very little about Sayeed – only that this was his first job out of university and that outside work Sayeed was keen on his nightlife and on sport, particularly rugby.

John, the Creator of Great Experiences, was, along with Sam, one of the oldest people on the payroll at DecisionMaker, with a solid track record of success in customer service. Sam knew that John was not really being stretched in his current role and wondered whether he was at risk of losing John to a headhunter.

Next came Chris. At twenty-eight, Chris was at the heart of DecisionMaker's age demographic. A hard worker, Chris was diligent in putting in the time required to get her work done and was very thorough. That work was product development, although Chris had enterprisingly styled herself DecisionMaker DaVinci. Sam thought about that for a while. It was a big role with a lot of scope, and one which could be quite critical to DecisionMaker's future.

Jane's chosen title was Busy Busy Work Work. She would have added 'Chop Chop Bang Bang' but thought such a long title was inefficient. In spite of her driving personality, Jane was very popular within the team, and her ambition had not appeared to cause a problem with Kathy. Sam wondered how Jane would feel about his promotion. Had she wanted the Ops Manager role herself – or did her plans lie elsewhere?

The final job title on Sam's chart was Rescue 'Services' – 'Debbie's' choice after joining from a rival organisation. It meant that Debbie attempted to find areas where systems broke down, or might break down, and then find ways to stop those things happening. All of which, thought Sam, was absolutely great. The problem was that as well as having lots of good ideas, Debbie also brought with her a tendency to talk fondly about how things were better in her previous company.

Sam was packing up for the day when Arnold Kramer telephoned and asked to see him. That was unusual. Perhaps Arnold did want to say something about his new appointment after all, or maybe the boss was more interested to know what he was doing in his new role.

'Sam,' Arnold began without any preamble, 'I've given you this job because I think you can do it.' Sam started to speak but Kramer raised a palm to silence him as he continued, 'and don't tell me you can't do it, because I can get someone at half your salary who can't do it!' Sam winced but said nothing. 'Your team needs sorting out. If Kathy hadn't gone I would have done something about it. As it is she has left us in the lurch at a very difficult time. We all need to pull together, Sam, but your team has really got to lift its game. We are missing deadlines and upsetting customers, no-one takes responsibility for anything and all I hear is that everything is someone else's fault. What you need to do,' Kramer pointed at Sam to emphasise his point, 'is get that team knuckled down, producing real results and efficiencies in the business, and really leading the way with attitude and great morale. I'm giving you a month, Sam, and I want to see results.'

CHAPTER 3

DILEMMA

Sam had plenty to think about on the train journey home. He knew he needed to get the team to step up, but how best to do that? A team meeting? Sam had been on the receiving end of supposedly inspirational rah-rah meetings. They were well-intentioned, and Sam was not a cynic by nature, but you didn't have to be a keen student of Dilbert to know such efforts usually fell flat at best. Besides, Sam had never seen himself as a great orator. He had good presentation skills but was more inclined to save those for the big occasions. With colleagues, Sam generally felt most comfortable one-to-one. So he couldn't quite see what he was going to say that would be powerful enough to transform the performance of the team. Pulling out his notebook he wrote down the names of the six team members, leaving a few blank lines underneath each one. Rosie, Sayeed, John, Chris, Jane and Debbie. And when the train pulled in at his station, he still had six names, each with a few blank lines underneath.

CHAPTER 4

HOME TRUTHS

Sam's wife Laura had a shorter commute home, on a good day at least. Today she had left the office at a reasonable time and with no significant delays she was home first, although not entirely soothed by having to stand all the way on the train. When Sam got in, Laura was in the kitchen with their daughter Emma and a certain amount of tension in the air.

'Hello darling. Hi Em,' he volunteered, trying to sound more cheerful than he felt. He didn't really need to wait for an answer before asking, 'Something wrong?' Two people speaking at once is never helpful, and as some wise person once said, it is always a mistake to lose two tempers in the same room. Sam held his hands over his ears in an exaggerated fashion, before saying, 'One at a time maybe?' That got him a sharp look from Laura, which cost her the split second she needed to get in first. Emma lost no time in taking advantage of the air time.

'I am going to get a tattoo. Mum says I'm not to, but I don't care. You can't tell me what to do for the rest of my life. Amelia has one, and so does Olivia, and you can't stop me, so stop trying!'

Laura looked up sharply: 'All yours Sam, I've had it. Over to you.'

'Well,' Sam played for time, 'OK – which doesn't mean I'm saying yes,' he countered quickly, 'but tell me, and your mother,' he added quickly, 'why do you want a tattoo?'

'Oh my god!' Emma rolled her eyes and shrugged her shoulders but Sam stayed with it. 'OK, OMG and all that, but I'd still like to know.'

'Because *everyone's* got one, that's why!'
'Everyone being Olivia and Amelia?'
'Obviously!'
'And who else?'
'I *don't know* who else! And I don't care.'
'OK, I think I am beginning to get the picture here. How about this? We don't talk about this just now.' Laura threw him another sharp look. 'Instead we all eat supper together and then we'll talk about tattoos tomorrow evening when everyone has had a chance to calm down.' Emma threw a huge shrug and planted both hands palms down on the kitchen table.

'Whatever!' she said very loudly, but that was the last talk of tattoos for that evening at least. The last family talk anyway. As soon as the plates were cleared away and Emma had disappeared to her room, Laura rounded on Sam.

'What was that all about? You're supposed to back me up. She is getting a tattoo over my dead body. I don't care what her friends are doing, Emma is too young to be making decisions like that.'

'What that was about was playing for time,' Sam responded. 'One thing that work has taught me over the years is that you can't have a sensible conversation with anyone who is angry or upset.'

'And twenty-four hours is going to change that?'

'Maybe and maybe not, but it will give us a chance to plan the kind of conversation we want to have with Emma, rather than simply being drawn into a shouting match where we just take up opposing positions.'

'Well I hope you have a good plan,' said Laura, reaching for the wine bottle. 'She's driving me to distraction just at the moment.'

At which point Sam's mobile rang, and in spite of Laura's roll of the eyes, he answered it.

CHAPTER 5

SAGE ADVICE

'Hi Bob, how's things?' Bob Rushmoor was a friend from university days. Sam and Bob had played rugby together, although neither of them had kept it up. They had been occasional gym buddies, and had trained together for a couple of charity bike rides. Bob was the legal counsel for a big international company, married with two teenage children. Sam didn't really think in terms of having a best friend, but if he had to name one, well, it would have been Bob.

'Good thanks, and you?'

Sam paused for a moment.

'Something wrong?' Bob asked.

'Oh no, not really. A bit of grief from Emma. She wants to get a tattoo.' Sam had wandered from the kitchen into his home office. He pushed the door closed behind him and dropped into the high-backed chair at his desk. 'Of course Laura doesn't want her to – well, actually I don't want her to either – but by the time I came in this evening they were well into it.'

'What did you do?'

'Postponed the conversation until tomorrow. Which saves having a row tonight but means I probably have one to look forward to.'

'Masterly!' said Bob. 'Time for tempers to cool and for you to plan the conversation.'

'Exactly what I thought. What do you think I should say to her?'

Bob laughed out loud. 'Absolutely no idea!' he responded.

'Well that's a great help,' said Sam. 'You mean to say that you've never had a tough conversation with Lily or Tania?'

'Oh sure, lots of them. But that doesn't mean I have a magic formula.'

'Not even with all that legal training? And they didn't teach you that on your MBA?'

'All law and spreadsheets,' Bob chuckled. 'Although I did a course when I was at Unacola that was really good on all that stuff. Of course it was aimed at the kind of conversations you have in business, not so much at home, but I have made some of it work here.'

'Now you are really intriguing me,' Sam chipped in. 'I haven't had a chance to tell you but I got promoted…'

'Hey, that's great news,' yelled Bob. 'That definitely calls for a drink. What did they make you, Head of Everything?'

'Not quite. Ops Manager. Kathy skedaddled along with the Ops Director and now I'm in charge of the team.'

'Good for you – well done, mate.'

'I'm not so sure,' Sam admitted. 'On the face of it, it's a good team, but they seem a bit all over the place now I am looking at the whole picture, and the good Dr Kramer ended the day on a high note by effectively charging me with sorting the whole company out in the space of a month.'

Bob whistled. 'Wow, tall order. Where do you reckon on starting?'

'Well, Rosie was first to barrel in with a whole load of ideas. She's my Workplace Evangelist – Facilities Coordinator really,' Sam added as he heard Bob snort.

'Well, ignoring the job title, although thinking about it maybe I should pitch for Righter of Mighty Wrongs Done Unto us by Others, but as I say, ignoring that, what is it you want Rosie to be doing for this next month?'

'Good question,' mused Sam. 'Things haven't being going too well generally; sales have slowed so Arnold and Dale are nervous about the investors, there have been a couple of big mistakes and some angry customers, and there is a bit of an atmosphere of blame around the place – something we never had until recently.'

'Hmm, OK.' Bob sounded thoughtful. 'So you don't want to get blamed for anything and you don't want Rosie to get blamed for anything, but you need to get her to produce a result.'

'That's it,' Sam agreed. 'Most of Rosie's big ideas are too big, or involve too many different decision-makers to even get started in a month. So it's got to be small things and quick wins – things that are visible and will have an impact.'

'Sounds good to me,' Bob agreed.

'So what did they teach you about that at Unacola?'

'Let me think about this for a second. Rosie is pretty keen, right?'

'Yes, she's full of beans and very bright, just a bit all over the place.'

'How about this then? You tell her the situation, without frightening the pants off her, obviously, and then ask her what she thinks a good goal would be for her over the next month.'

'Sounds good,' Sam agreed.

'Now of course you may not think that what she comes up with is a good goal. If that's the case, just hold on to your horses and ask how achievable it will be, whether it will get her where you both need her to be, and keep going until she really has got a good goal, or a set of goals.'

'OK...' Sam sounded thoughtful.

'Hang on, I haven't finished yet,' Bob went on. 'You need to anchor those goals in reality. It's like the old joke: "How do I get to Cornwall? Well if I were you, I wouldn't start from here." Here is where we all are. So get her to work out where she is starting from, and maybe what she is up against before you go any further.'

'OK.' Sam had pulled his keyboard forwards and was tapping out notes as he listened. 'What then?'

'Well, you are going to have a lot on your plate, so you are going to need her to take ownership of this stuff, and the best way to do that is to ask her how she thinks she could get from here to there.'

'Makes sense.'

'Ah, but there's a trick to this bit – and this really has stood me in good stead. Get her to give you a number of options. Don't take her first suggestion. The more you can work this bit the better result you are likely to get.'

'Right, so it's like an idea generation thing?' asked Sam.

'Yes, in a way, but remember, she'll be doing all the generating. Your job is simply to get Rosie to think of lots of different ways, and then have her choose the best one.' Bob paused and then chipped in again, 'Oh, and one more thing. You are going to want to know how she's doing, but if you keep going and asking her she'll feel like you're trying to manage her all the time. Get her to tell you when she is going to report back and how.'

'Right, you're on,' affirmed Sam. 'That's my conversation with Rosie. Now what about Emma?'

'Still no idea there!' Bob laughed. 'Now, after all that, the real reason I called is to see whether you and Laura will come over next weekend? It's been too long. Come for lunch on Sunday – and bring Emma, if she'll come.'

CHAPTER 6

TOM, HUCK AND MARK

Sam had a bad night's sleep. His team kept floating in and out of his dreams. In confused images Sayeed and Rosie appeared tattooed like Maori warriors. Debbie, Jane and Chris came on as a backing group singing 'You'll never work again' to the tune of 'You'll Never Walk Alone'. John seemed to always be waving from a distance. Every time Sam tried to speak to any of them they melted away, only to come back again. Again and again he tried to have the same conversations: the business performance, Dr Kramer, what we all need to do…

At five o'clock, Sam gave up the unequal struggle, slid out of the bed, thankfully without disturbing Laura, grabbed his dressing gown from the back of the bedroom door and crept downstairs. He was still sitting at the kitchen table, brooding over a mug of tea, when he suddenly realised what his subconscious had been trying to tell him for the past few hours.

In one small moment of quiet genius, he suddenly understood that he needed to have a completely different conversation with everyone in the team if he was to make the difference that Kramer demanded and that the company so badly needed.

Over the usual hasty breakfast some time later, he tried to explain it to Laura.

'You remember Mark Twain? You know, Tom Sawyer, Huckleberry Finn, and all that?'

'Never read him,' said Laura, messaging on her phone and munching toast at the same time.

'When you've got a hammer in your hand, an awful lot of things look like nails!' said Sam.

'Sorry?'

'Mark Twain is supposed to have said that. He's saying when you've only got one solution, one way of thinking about things, you try to apply that to everything, no matter whether it's appropriate or not. It suddenly occurred to me that most of the managers I've worked for only ever seemed to have one conversation, whatever the circumstances.'

'And that's the point about the hammer and the nails?'

'Exactly. The conversation has always been about the numbers, what we need to do and all that stuff.'

'I can definitely associate with that,' said Laura, gulping a last mouthful of tea, 'and I'm pretty sure that conversation will be coming my way at some point today if I don't get myself into the office and get some stuff done.'

'My point, precisely,' said Sam, following her to the door. 'But I need to have a different conversation with everyone in my team.'

'Bye,' Laura waved as she jumped into her car and headed off.

'I just wish I knew how to do that,' thought Sam as he headed for the station.

CHAPTER 7

COACHING
(Conversation #1: 'What can you do about that?')

Sam was in early. Enthused with his new idea, he had used his commute to jot down some notes from his phone call with Bob the night before and map out a rough structure for his conversation with Rosie. It seemed to settle in to four parts, with a natural flow between them. The first would be to ask Rosie what she wanted to achieve, how she saw her goals and objectives, and perhaps to ask her to put those into a broader context before going down into the detail. The second part was more of a reality check. After all, Sam thought to himself, I could set myself an objective to win the Men's 400 Metre Hurdles Final at the next Olympics. The only problem is, my best time for 400 metres, which was when I was at school twenty years ago, was about sixty seconds, and the world record for the event is about forty-seven seconds – and I have never hurdled in my life! So checking where we are now in relation to the goal could be useful.

The part of his conversation with Bob that had really been intriguing was the idea of options. Sam was pretty used to the idea of setting a goal, making a plan to reach it, and setting off in hot pursuit of it. Pausing to deliberately create and then weigh up some different ways of getting to the goal was a new and interesting idea. He would explore that with Rosie, but, remembering Bob's injunction about how to have the conversation, he would only do that by asking her questions.

Lastly, he was also quite taken with the idea of asking Rosie to confirm back to him what she was going to do and when. Every team leader and manager Sam had ever had had simply told him what their expectations were about reporting back. That didn't mean they had been rude or authoritative about it, rather they had always said something like: 'Let me know how you're doing by the end of the week.' Sam was intrigued by the idea of asking Rosie when she would report back, and how. It seemed to him that this strategy left all the responsibility with Rosie – and for that reason it was more likely to produce a good result.

At the office Sam checked in with Rosie and managed to get a meeting room booked for 11.30 a.m. DecisionMaker was not big on meeting rooms. Most people used the open areas, or went out to local coffee shops, but there were a couple of rooms and Sam booked the smaller one for an hour. Rosie bounced in promptly, put down a brightly coloured notebook and a coffee from the fancy machine in the kitchen area and looked expectantly at Sam.

'What's on your mind, boss?' she asked with a grin.

'Well, I think we can just stick with Sam, like we always have,' he responded with a smile.

'Just kidding,' replied Rosie and reached for her coffee.

Reminding himself to set the scene by starting with the context, Sam began.

'As you know, things haven't been great lately. I'm not talking about our team,' he covered quickly, 'just' overall. Arnold thinks we could be doing more. Actually, he thinks we definitely should be doing more, to help the rest of the organisation. Getting people to work a bit better together, making sure we don't drop the ball, being more efficient.'

'Business as usual then?' chipped in Rosie.

'Well yes – but we need a bit more than that – BusinessPlus, you might call it.'

'Hey I like that!' Rosie opened her notebook and jotted down the words 'BusinessPlus' at the top of a new page. 'How are we going to do that?'

'Well, there's a bit more. We not only have to show we are doing more to benefit the business than we have been. We have to start to make that pretty obvious within a month. Which is not long.'

'Wow. You're telling me. So what's the plan?'

'The plan is,' grinned Sam, 'for you to tell me what you think would be a couple of great goals for you this month. What do you think you can deliver that people will really appreciate and talk about, and will have a visible effect?'

Rosie frowned. 'Hmm. Starting with the easy ones, eh?' She turned back a couple of pages in her notebook. 'I brought my list of Top Ten Things – and there are a couple of quick wins in there. High-impact quick wins might be more of a challenge though.'

'Well, let's give it a shot. What have you got?'

'OK, idea number one,' Rosie paused for a moment, her pen hovering over her list. 'No, actually scrub that,' she said. 'We can come back to that one.'

Sam said nothing, but noted that handing the baton over to Rosie had actually made her reassess some of her ideas rather than fire-hosing him with all of them at once.

'There are a couple of things that are really hacking people off,' Rosie said more thoughtfully. 'I'm not saying fixing those would massively impact performance, or even motivate anyone much, but they would stop a lot of griping.'

'OK, that sounds like a good place to start. What are they?'

'Well, lockers, for one. Some people would like an extra locker, for gym kit or cycling gear, that kind of thing. And we should have enough to go round, but there's a whole bunch of them being used for document storage.'

'Why's that?'

'Well, when there were a lot spare I think someone just decided it would save storing stuff offsite, so they used a few, and then a few more. There are at least ten or twelve we could free up.'

'And would that be enough for everyone who wants extra locker space?'

'It would be more than enough for everyone who has asked me about it.'

'So whose documents are in the lockers?'

'I'd have to check that, they're locked after all,' Rosie laughed. 'I'm pretty sure some of it is finance stuff. It can't be that important though, because otherwise they would have put it into proper secure storage. I can ask around and find out.'

'OK, what are you saying the goal is here?'

'Well, the quick win is that people who want extra locker space for gym kit and so on can have it, and that'll be one less source of discontent around the place.'

'Do other people want more locker space for other things?'

'Not that I'm aware of, but I can check. That's a good point, actually. I wouldn't want to be accused of favouring the gym-bunnies over anyone else.'

Sam thought so too and said as much. 'Just before you leap into action over the lockers,' he said, looking down at the notes he had made from his chat with Bob on the phone the night before, 'how else could you sort out the gym kit problem? Suppose you can't get an agreement to free up those lockers? What then?'

Rosie thought for a moment. 'Most people have their stuff in a separate bag, I think. They tuck the bag, under their workstation, or wherever they happen to be working, then Arnold or Dale walk by and remind them we are not supposed to have any clutter around and everything should be in a locker!'

'So where does that leave us? Or, better question,' Sam added quickly, 'where does that *take* us?'

'No chance of changing the policy, that's for sure.' Rosie paused again, frowning. 'We could perhaps get an agreement for people to leave their bags in the locker area. There is a space there we could mark as a Bag Drop. We could ask everyone to put an ID tag on their bags so we would know who has got stuff there. Even better, we could create and issue the tags so they would be immediately identifiable.'

'Good idea,' noted Sam. 'Third option?'

'Umm, I don't think I have one right now.'

'Well, let's go with what we have,' suggested Sam, thinking it was time to move on from lockers. 'Which one do you prefer?'

'Oh the first one, definitely.'

'So what will you do – what's you first action going to be?'

'I'm going to find out what is actually in those lockers. After all, given my job, I really ought to know anyway. I'll start with Finance and move on to HR. I always wanted to be a detective,' Rosie laughed.

'Good. What's next on the agenda?'

At the end of an hour they had repeated the same process twice more, and having explored a number of options for how to achieve each one, Rosie had three clear goals, each with a plan beginning with a simple first action, and an agreement about keeping Sam up to date with progress.

'Thanks, Sam,' said Rosie as they left the meeting room. 'Great coaching session.'

'Coaching session?' queried Sam.

Rosie turned to face him with a big smile. 'Come on – I sussed you out! That was coaching!'

'In what way?'

'Well, you asked me what my goal was, or at least got me to pick one from my list – which is good for me because usually I try to do everything at once. Then you checked out what the situation actually is – where I am with things. Then you asked me to create some options around it, and got me to choose one and say what I will do. What I am *actually* going to do about it. Oh, and when I'm going to tell you I've done it.'

'Yeah, I can see that,' said Sam a little uncertainly.

'I went on a training course on it years ago,' Rosie laughed. 'Sounds as though you figured it out for yourself.'

'Well, something like that.' Sam was thinking more about what he was going to say to Bob Rushmoor when he called him back that evening.

'Works for me,' called Rosie as she headed off. 'Thanks again.'

Sam pulled out his phone and googled Coaching – and there it all was. What the other person wants to do, where they are now, how they could do it and what they are prepared to do about it. Coupled with the idea of just asking questions, no telling, and no giving advice. 'Well, I have a couple of questions for Mr Rushmoor,' thought Sam. But he had to admit he was more inclined to chuckle than to swear about it. 'Cunning old so-and-so,' he thought. 'He really pulled one on me there, getting me to do it, rather than just telling me about it.'

* * * * *

'Experience first, learning after – that's my rule!' was Bob's retort after Sam had finished describing his conversation with Rosie.

'Well, yes. I did think afterwards I might have looked a bit of an idiot.'

'Not much chance of that after you got a great result for Rosie – and for you I might add. And I knew you would.'

'I still think I was lucky,' grumbled Sam.

'Ah, but you never used to believe in luck, did you? So that's interesting. See you at the weekend.'

With that Bob hung up, leaving Sam to ponder on luck, his conversation with Rosie, and what else Bob might know that he didn't.

CHAPTER 8

ACCOUNTABILITY
Conversation #2: 'Who should really own this?'

A few days later, Sayeed's monthly cost forecast landed on Sam's desk. Although it was always referred to as the Cost Forecast in Operations, it was really more of a prediction of how the next month would look against budget, and where needs not covered in the budget might crop up. Sam went through the figures, and then again with increasing alarm. He was about to call Sayeed and then paused. Sayeed's job was primarily to work on analysing historical purchasing costs, forecasting future costs, and finding prospective suppliers. Apart from that Sam knew very little about Sayeed's role, or how Sayeed went about his work. He remembered that this was Sayeed's first job after leaving university, and the thought played on his mind.

'What sort of conversation do I want to have here?' he wondered, and answered himself almost immediately. 'I need this to be positive. I don't want to de-motivate him, but I do need to sort some things out.' In this case, starting with Sayeed's goals was not going to work. 'I need to understand more,' he thought. Reaching for his notepad he wrote: 'What's going on?' Realising straight away that just asking that would be heading for trouble, he added a dash and the words 'tell me more.'

The next step, he decided, would be to find out exactly how Sayeed had arrived at his report, and incidentally why he thought it was OK to send the report to Sam without any warning, introduction or suggestions of what they might do about it. Underneath 'What's going on?' he wrote: 'How come?' Not very elegant, he acknowledged to himself, but it would do for now. After a moment or two he added a dash to that as well and the words 'no blame!'

OK, Sam reasoned, if we can get that far I'll know where Sayeed got his information from and how he put the report together. I'll also understand why he doesn't seem to be taking any ownership of it. Then I'll need to get him to understand what I really need from him, and how I want him to work. Starting a third line on his notepad, he wrote: 'What can we do about this?'

Sam thought back to his conversation with Rosie. The bit at the end where he had asked her what she was going to do had worked really well. Here, it seemed they would cover what needed doing in the third part of the conversation. The goal was how to get Sayeed to see that it was his job to do these things. In a sudden moment of clarity, and feeling rather pleased with himself, Sam wrote: 'Who?' on the fourth line and headed for the coffee machine.

This conversation, he felt, might go better in a more relaxed setting. At least as many DecisionMaker meetings took place in local coffee shops and hotels as in the office, so suggesting to Sayeed that they head off for a chat outside was natural and normal. The area was buzzing. Not just with people on the streets but with construction all around. Two five-star hotels were going up within a few short steps of DecisionMaker's offices, and all around older buildings were being converted, modernised and hardwired to cope with the rapid influx of new businesses wanting to tap into the energy and into the talent pool being swept into the area. Sam and Sayeed found a table in one of the quieter coffee bars where the coffee was good but not yet deconstructed and where they could talk sensibly.

'I'm a bit concerned about the latest cost forecast,' Sam began. Sayeed put down his coffee and cocked his head inquiringly. 'Tell me a bit more about it. How do you put these together?'

'Well,' Sayeed looked thoughtful, 'you know I never really had any training in how to do it so I sort of had to make it up as I went along.' Sayeed smiled and shrugged. 'OK, so I started out by going around and checking with people what they thought might come up that could be outside budget – then I realised I was just giving people an opportunity to give me a shopping list. So I stopped doing that.'

'And…?' prompted Sam.

'Well,' Sayeed paused, looking rather uncomfortable. 'I don't want to say I just started making it up,' he started, and then stopped again, glancing up at Sam with some apprehension.

'I think you've just answered my second question,' said Sam. Sayeed looked equally curious and perturbed. 'Don't panic,' Sam continued, lifting a hand, 'this is not blame – I just want to know what the situation is, and how we got to be here. I mean, if the cost forecast is really accurate I ought to be running cap-in-hand to Finance to try and sort things out before Arnold finds out and comes gunning for me. Which, if you think about it, is no way to run a business.'

Sayeed sighed. 'No,' he said, 'obviously.'

'So, I think what you're saying is that you weren't really shown how to do this properly, you've had to make it up a bit as you've gone along, and the current cost forecast, which is the only one I am actually interested in at the moment, isn't really accurate?'

'No, it's not' agreed Sayeed quietly, 'but I don't know what the right answer is.' He looked downcast.

'Great!' Sam's exclamation startled Sayeed.

'Sorry?' Sayeed responded. 'What's great about this?'

'Well now we know where we are, we can do something about it.'

Sayeed was slightly taken aback by Sam's evident good humour. 'I thought you'd put me on a warning at the very least,' he admitted ruefully.

'Come on,' Sam replied, 'if I thought you couldn't do it that would be different. This is about all of us being accountable. It's about doing what we say we will, and owning up when we don't know rather than trying to bluff things out.'

'Hmm.' Sayeed looked up. 'People don't seem to talk much about accountability at DecisionMaker, do they?'

'Well we're going to be talking about it from now on,' Sam confirmed. 'If we are going to deliver what Arnold wants – and he wants to see results in a month…'

'In a month? You're joking aren't you?'

'Most definitely not, I'm afraid. Arnold has given me one month to show tangible results. I think his actual phrase was "real results and efficiencies in the business and really leading the way with attitude and great morale".'

'Real results and efficiencies, leading with attitude and great morale,' Sayeed played back. 'That's a pretty good strapline for the team you know – we should use that.'

'You might be right there,' Sam allowed, 'I hadn't thought of that. Actually, I had taken it as somewhere between a challenge and a threat,' he went on, 'but we could make it an aspiration.'

'Or even a deliverable,' added Sayeed thoughtfully.

Sam realised that the conversation had taken quite a positive turn, but at the same time it was drifting away from his original purpose, and he didn't want to be distracted.

'Let's come back to that,' he said. 'What I want to do in this conversation is make sure we are both absolutely clear what the deliverable is on the cost forecast.'

Sayeed drank the last of his coffee and put the mug down. 'I have to produce an accurate monthly forecast, or at least one that is as accurate as I can make it.'

'And is that all?'

'No, I get it, I also have to put a commentary or some analysis on to it that points out where the figures have come from, together with some estimate of how accurate I think they are likely to be.'

'That would be good,' agreed Sam. 'Do you mind my asking why you haven't been doing that up to now?'

Sayeed looked a bit sheepish and said quietly, 'I thought if I just produced the figures I could always blame someone else if the forecast wasn't good.'

'Whereas if you do a proper job, saying where the figures came from, adding your commentary and so on, then it's all your fault if the forecast is wrong?'

'Yup, that's pretty much it, I guess.'

Sam grinned and made sure Sayeed saw it. 'Do you ever come to work to get blamed?' he asked.

'Sorry?' Sayeed looked up, surprised.

'Do you ever come to work in order to be blamed for something?' Sam repeated.

Sayeed laughed. 'No, of course not!'

'Do you think anyone gets up in the morning, looks in the mirror and says to themselves, "I think I'll go to work today and do some really stupid things so that I can get blamed for making mistakes. That should be fun and make sure I have a good day"?'

'No, of course not!' Sayeed was back to looking puzzled. 'What are you getting at?'

'No-one goes to work to get blamed, Sayeed. And I'm not in the business of blame. I do want a great cost forecast every month though, and I want you to provide it. Complete with analysis, commentary, threats and opportunities and all that good stuff.'

Sayeed nodded and drew a deep breath. 'OK.'

'It won't be right first time, it'll never be perfect, because it's a forecast, but as long as you stand by it, and you can tell me and other people how you arrived at the figures, and why, then I will not only not blame you myself – because I wouldn't anyway,' Sam added hastily, 'but I will also defend you and the forecast to anyone else who may take issue with it.'

'Including Dr Kramer?'

'Most definitely including our noble leader,' Sam confirmed. 'So, all clear?'

'Definitely,' Sayeed nodded again. 'Just one thing. There are some areas I am really not sure how to deal with. Can I come to you for some help on those?'

'Yes, of course.' Sam thought quickly. It was important that Sayeed should have help when he needed it, but equally important that Sam should not end up solving Sayeed's problems for him. 'A couple of things on that though. If you want to ask me about something to do with any of this, come and see me, but make sure we mark out time for it. Fifteen minutes, half an hour, whatever you think, just don't spring a problem on me when I'm in the middle of something else or on my way into a meeting.'

'OK.' Sayeed pulled out his phone and tapped in a note. 'Problems by appointment only,' he said out loud.

'Yes, and at no time is your problem going to become my problem,' Sam went on.

Sayeed raised his eyebrows slightly at that one, but tapped into his phone again, saying, 'My problems stay my problems.'

'Well, they only stay problems until you've solved them,' said Sam, 'they just don't become my problems. After all, a moment ago, you asked whether you can come for help if you have any problems. If you hand them back to me, and I take them off you, then they're not your problems any more, are they? And if you don't have a problem then I can't help you.'

That brought a wry smile to Sayeed's face. 'Wow,' he said after thinking it over for a moment. 'I see what you mean. I had never thought about that. I think I just learned something else about accountability.'

'That doesn't mean I am going to leave you in the lurch,' Sam pointed out. 'It means that I will work with you to help you find ways to solve any problems you have, and you will then go off and take the necessary actions. We can agree what you are going to do, and how far you can go, every time, so you can be sure what you've got my authority for and what you haven't.'

'Cool,' confirmed Sayeed. 'That sounds good.' There was a short pause. 'Feels like it's time to get back to work,' he ventured after a moment.

'Sounds good to me,' agreed Sam, and they headed back to the office.

CHAPTER 9

MORE THAN ONE WAY

Sunday at the Rushmoor's was something of a treat for Sam and Laura. Laura got on well with Bob's wife Jean and the conversation, both before and after lunch, often separated along gender lines, with the two women more interested in children and family affairs while Bob and Sam always seemed to float back to business, wherever the conversation started.

Jean was a good cook and the shoulder of lamb she had roasting when Sam and Laura arrived was well-seasoned with rosemary and sitting on a bed of onions and garlic, filling the kitchen with a mouth-watering aroma and the guests with a sense of anticipation. Bob served drinks and he and Sam happily agreed to the suggestion that they should stop cluttering up the kitchen and go and sit somewhere else.

'I have a bone to pick with you,' Sam said cheerfully, raising his glass.

'Cheers,' responded Bob. 'What have I done?'

'Coaching. You told me how to do it – you didn't tell me it was a well-known way to do it!'

Bob chuckled. 'And your point, exactly?'

'Well, for a start, at the end of the conversation, note that – at the *end* of the conversation – Rosie explained it back to me!'

'And did that matter?'

'Actually, no. It didn't seem to matter at all.'

'I knew it wouldn't! The only time you are ever going to upset someone doing that is if they are completely unwilling, or if they really don't know what they are doing. In which case coaching is unlikely to work.'

'Even so...' admonished Sam.

'Experience first, learning after – that's my motto,' Bob laughed.

'Hmm, I shall be watching out for you in future,' said Sam. 'What was that you just said about people who aren't willing?'

'Oh well, I always say imagine trying to coach a reluctant teenager? You'd have a conversation that went something like: "What's your goal?" "Dunno, whatever" – and that would be the end of that!'

Sam thought back to his chat with Emma on the subject of tattoos and was about to say something rather smug when Laura put her head round the door to say that Jean was asking them to come to the table.

The lamb was served with new potatoes and lots of fresh vegetables, and followed by a fruit pie. After a brief discussion before the second glass of wine, Laura graciously offered to switch to water and be their driver for the journey home, and Sam actually relaxed for what felt like the first time in a week.

'I think I may have found another kind of conversation,' he remarked to Bob as they carried their coffee through to the living room after lunch.

'Oh really?' Bob looked interested. 'Tell me about it.'

'Well,' said Sam, 'I started from first principles you might say. I worked out what I thought the problem was, and then where I should start and finish the conversation in order to get to where I wanted to be – and where I wanted the other person to be.'

'And did that work for both of you?'

'Yes, it did. It was really about getting someone to be properly accountable for something, and it seemed to work very well.'

'So how did your conversation go?'

'I started by asking what he thought the situation was – a kind of "what's happening?" or "where are we?"'

'Always good to get that sorted out – or at least come to an agreement about it,' Bob chuckled.

'Agreed,' said Sam, 'but then I wanted to know how come? I mean, how did we get to be here?'

'Good move, but I am thinking that would have to be handled quite carefully.'

'Yes, the aim was just to find out how we could stop the same thing happening again. So I wrote myself a little reminder that said "no blame" and I made it very clear that was not what it was about.'

'I like it a lot so far,' Bob chipped in. 'What came next?'

'I asked what we could do about it.'

'OK, but I thought you wanted the other person to take this thing on, not to get you involved in it again?'

'Oh, too right,' Sam agreed. 'So I made sure the last part was "who?" meaning "who is doing this, you or me?" And I made it clear that in this case I would be available for help and advice only "by appointment", so to speak, and most definitely not to start taking problems back.'

'Well that sounds pretty cute,' said Bob. 'The Accountability Conversation.' He laughed. 'You should trademark that!'

Sam smiled. 'I think I'd rather just share it. I think one of the problems we have at DecisionMaker is a lack of clear accountability. It's not that people are deliberately trying to duck things, it's just that it's too easy for people to slide away from things they have promised to deliver. I don't want a culture where people get yelled at if they don't do what they say.'

'Yeah, fear may work in the short term,' Bob came in, 'but in my experience, it's pretty corrosive over time. Good people won't put up with it so you end up with a business made up of bullies and victims and that doesn't usually work too well.'

'No, and speaking of that, I am quite concerned that it's going that way a bit at the top. I don't know what's eating Arnold Kramer but he's got a real bee in his bonnet about something at the moment.'

As it turned out, Sam did not have long to wait to find out exactly what was on Dr Kramer's mind.

CHAPTER 10

BLUE MONDAY

Sam's cheerful outlook for the week ahead lasted just five minutes into Monday morning, by which time John had messaged to say he was not well and would not be coming in, Jane was visibly fuming about something, and he had a directive to see Dr Kramer. Now.

As well as Dr Kramer, Sam found Dale Howson looking worried, and Gordon Blaine, the Sales Director, looking tight-lipped and grim. Sam took the vacant chair, took in the atmosphere in the room, and wondered what the hell he had missed while he had been busy checking his emails, Slack, his messages and his newsfeeds on the way in that morning. It soon transpired that Exigenta was what he had missed, but only because they had been trying to hush things up until their CEO could speak directly to Arnold Kramer. That conversation, Sam quickly realised, had not been a pleasant experience.

Exigenta was a huge private equity firm. Meaning that it took money from other investment businesses and wealthy individuals and invested it directly into businesses, often adding its own management. The investment might be used to turn around a failing business, to invest in new technology or a business transformation, or to provide liquidity for a flotation or sale. The firm was notoriously secretive, having been attacked in the press and online for the level of its income and earnings and the sky-high salaries reportedly being paid to senior people there.

With a portfolio of around eighty companies employing over half a million people around the world, and combined revenues of tens of millions of dollars, these were not people who threw money around.

They were people who were used to making big decisions – and making good decisions. The fact that they had signed up as a DecisionMaker customer had been a very big deal. The fact that no-one was supposed to know that, and that somehow the news had leaked out, had already caused one major bust-up between the two companies. This, it turned out, was much, much worse.

One of the businesses Exigenta was invested in had recently hit the headlines, and not in a good way. The business decommissioned radiotherapy sources that had passed their useful life in hospitals, and their plant had suffered a break-in. The suspected motive was not any of the radioactive materials themselves, and the business was strenuously denying that any radioactive materials were unaccounted for. Instead, it was suggested that the thieves had been after the highly valuable metal used in the construction and shielding of the units. What was lighting up the internet was the suggestion that this haul of scrap metal might in itself contain potentially lethal levels of radioactivity. Even to a non-expert like Sam this seemed highly unlikely, but lack of likelihood never stopped a good viral rumour.

Arnold Kramer explained all of this tersely, barely looking up at Sam, who was beginning to wonder what all this had to do with DecisionMaker, let alone with him, when Dr Kramer dropped the bombshell.

'So what is now doing the rounds,' he looked up at last and stared across his desk directly at Sam, 'is a brilliant piece of satire wondering how clever people like those at Exigenta managed to make such a daft decision as to invest in RRI in the first place…'

'RRI?' asked Sam, fully expecting a rebuke for the interruption but unwilling to keep wading further into things he really knew nothing about.

'Radiotherapy Reclamations International,' muttered Gordon Blaine, collecting the irritated stare from Dr Kramer that Sam had been expecting to come his way.

'...and suggesting that using our software may well be the cause of their problem,' Dr Kramer finished icily. Sam was saved from having to respond immediately as Sophie Ayar, DecisionMaker's Head of Communications, entered the room apologising.

'Sorry, sorry, sorry,' she began before sensing the atmosphere in the room and falling silent.

'The point is,' Dr Kramer continued, like a battleship ploughing through arctic waters, 'that in precisely three weeks' time, we pitch for our next funding round.' His steely gaze swept around the room, from Sophie to Sam, on to Gordon and then back again. Dale Howson, Sam noted, escaped the glare but looked uncomfortable nonetheless.

'I want to know where that piece of pseudo-reportage came from,' he told Sophie, who nodded quickly. Sam guessed she had been late because she had been trying to arm herself with answers before joining the meeting and was probably well up with what had been going on.

'Gordon, please reassure all our other customers that this is all a piece of arrant nonsense which will be immediately refuted as soon as we have all the facts. Reassure them of the absolute credentials of the tool and do not let any of them even *think* of defecting to an inferior rival, there being no equal ones,' he added for good measure, 'and then come back here and reassure me that they have all believed you. Lock, stock and barrel.'

'Sam,' Kramer barked, and Sam braced himself for the onslaught. 'I am saying just two words to you,' and Arnold said them very slowly: 'Customer Satisfaction.' Sam nodded, ducking his head quickly to hide a nervous swallow. Dr Kramer waved his right hand across the desk in a sweeping motion, broadly directing them all to the door. Sophie was first out, but only because Sam stood back to let her. Gordon passed them both outside muttering 'Good luck,' as his long legs swept him away, phone in hand.

CHAPTER 11

IN IT TOGETHER

Sam managed to grab one of DecisionMaker's few meeting rooms and called the team together. Perhaps a bit too hastily, he thought. He hadn't really worked out what he wanted to say to them, and suddenly realised he was in danger of simply spreading doom and gloom along with the bad news. In the nick of time he remembered something Laura's father had always done when presented with bad news. He would somehow find a way to turn it on its head, to look on the bright side, as he used to say. What was great about this though? Sam wondered. Then he had a flash of inspiration.

The team was slow assembling. Rosie and Debbie arrived first, followed by Chris. Sayeed arrived a few moments later looking quizzical and not saying much. A good five minutes of chat ensued before Jane came through the door, dropped her notebook on to the table with a bang and slumped into a chair. Sam was tempted to ask what was wrong but decided, wisely, that he wasn't going to let a bit of bad behaviour at the start derail the meeting.

'When I was given this job, Arnold Kramer told me he wanted to see results within a month. Now a month is not very long and I wasn't at all sure how we were going to accomplish anything very impactful in that time. But we have just been given a great opportunity.' There were puzzled looks around the table. Even if the impact of the RRI story wasn't obvious at this stage, it had been obvious to all that something was wrong as they had arrived.

Sam outlined the situation without pulling any punches, but equally without making any unfounded predictions.

'So what's it got to do with us?' asked Jane with a shrug. 'Not much any of us can do about that is there? It's just a load of idiot trolls on the web. That's Sophie Ayar's job.'

'And I'm sure Sophie is on the case,' Sam cut in coolly. 'She was in the meeting this morning and I expect she is briefing her team right now. What I am interested in is deciding on some really good actions *we* can take as a team, that will help in this situation and reflect well on all of us.' Sam was not the only one to notice Jane roll her eyes at that and was grateful when Debbie chipped in.

'It's a shame John's not here.' Debbie had something of a habit of stating the obvious. 'Does anyone know what's wrong with him?'

'Only that he said he wouldn't be in today,' replied Chris.

'Let's assume he won't be in for a few days,' suggested Sam, 'and work out what we can do without him being here.'

'Sorry to play the one-note-samba,' Jane came in, without sounding sorry at all, 'but my role is concerned with how we process things efficiently, a bit of who does what and improving processes. What am I supposed to do about the fact that Exigenta bought a company that recycles nuclear thingummies from hospitals, and their security is obviously horribly slack and they have been broken into?'

'Hang on, that's a good point.' Sayeed leaned forward towards Jane, spreading his arms across the table. 'When did Exigenta buy into RRI? Was that after they started using our software, or sometime before?'

'That is a good point,' added Chris, 'and, thinking about it, do we know whether they use our software to actually inform their investment decisions, or…' she tailed off indecisively.

'Or what?' asked Jane, with a degree of sarcasm.

'Or perhaps for making management decisions inside their portfolio companies,' Sam finished. 'That's a really good point, Chris. I'll have a word with Gordon. I'm guessing that's not the case or he would have mentioned it this morning as a quick way of killing all the bad publicity, but we should check.'

'I'm going to get myself around a bit and find out what everyone is saying.' Rosie tapped the table firmly with her finger. 'I've got to say, Sam, that whenever people see long faces coming out of a meeting with Arnold the rumour mill goes into overdrive.'

'That's silly,' said Sayeed, then quickly added, 'not you Rosie, I meant it's silly of people to be deflected so easily.'

'Normal though,' said Rosie. 'If we don't get the big story straight away from the top, then everyone starts to make up their own little stories. Which is sort of what's happening with this whole RRI thing anyway. So our job is to get people telling positive stories. I'm going to remind everyone what a great place DecisionMaker is to work. After all, it is my job to make it a great place to work,' she finished triumphantly.

'Well, I guess I can do that too,' said Sayeed. 'In fact, that's something we can *all* do.'

CHAPTER 12

KUDOS

Sam's first action on leaving the meeting was to go and see Gordon Blaine, but it would not be true to say that was his first thought. His thoughts were occupied by what to do about Jane. Just when he needed the whole team to pull together and use the opportunity to make a bit of a mark, Jane was acting like a complete saboteur. What was it that got into people? Fortunately, before he could focus all of his attention on how disruptive Jane had been, he arrived in Sales and found Gordon straight away.

'Gordon, sorry to bother you, and I know you've probably got this covered, but I've just come from a team meeting where Sayeed Ahmed asked a really good question,' Sam began.

'Did he, indeed? And what might that have been, under our current circumstances?' he asked in his Scottish accent, but not without a hint of a smile.

'He asked when Exigenta actually bought into RRI,' Sam filled in quickly. 'He was thinking about whether it was after they started using our software or before.'

'Well, you are right,' Gordon confirmed, 'that had occurred to me as well. It turns out it was around about the same time.'

'Not so helpful, then,' admitted Sam. 'There was another question though, and that was whether they actually use DecisionMaker software to inform their investment decisions or only for management decisions in the portfolio companies?'

'I'm beginning to think we should be making much more use of your team, Sam,' Gordon smiled. 'To be fair, I'd had exactly the same thought myself, but I am impressed that Operations would be thinking so creatively!'

Sam ignored the apparent slight and stayed on track. 'And…?' he asked.

'If I could get hold of any of my contacts at Exigenta I could probably answer that question for you, but they are doing a very good impression of a group of people who do not want to talk to me at the moment,' Gordon shrugged and spread his hands in a 'what can you do?' manner.

Sam was about to go when, sensing that he might have gained a little bit of kudos by at least coming with the idea, he paused.

'Gordon, can I change the subject completely?' he asked.

Gordon nodded and said, 'Why not? It's all happening today, isn't it?'

'So I told you I had just come from a team meeting. Someone, and I'm not saying who, was behaving very badly. You must have come across this before…'

Gordon rolled his eyes. 'Just once or twice in my long and illustrious, and possibly soon to be over, career.'

'Come on, Arnold's not going to sack you over this!' Sam protested.

'Well, probably not,' Gordon admitted. 'What do you want to know, laddie?'

'Very simply, what's the best way to deal with that?'

'Ah, now that I *can* tell you,' Gordon said with a grin. 'First of all, take it offline. Don't say anything in public, unless you absolutely have to stop someone dead in their tracks. And even then, don't say any more than you need to in order to stop them. There's no telling the havoc you can wreak with a bit of public humiliation.' He paused and shook his head. Sam said nothing.

'So,' continued Gordon, 'here's my formula. It came from a man I respected very much and who taught me a great deal – and it has stood me in good stead.'

'First,' he went on, 'state the problem. You have to tell them,' and here Gordon raised an index finger to emphasise the point, 'unequivocally what you are there to talk about. Don't shy away from that or you'll be lost before you've begun.' Sam nodded.

Gordon went on. 'Second, you need to say *why* it is a problem. You have to accept that some people just don't understand the effect they are having on others.' He paused and then continued. 'But leaving this morning's meeting with Arnold aside, I would suggest that you say what you expect, whether that's in terms of performance, behaviour, attitude, or whatever it may be.'

'So far, so good,' Sam chipped in, feeling more confident.

'Aye well, that's as may be,' Gordon came back, 'but now I think I may be about to surprise you a wee bit. Ask for *their* perspective.' Sam nodded, not quite comprehending, but let Gordon go on.

'Ask them for their view of the situation. And when you've done that, and no contradicting them, mind, ask for their solution.'

'I must say,' Sam said thoughtfully, 'I hadn't thought of that.'

'Well you might be surprised if you try it,' Gordon went on. 'It has been my experience that on many occasions the other person's solution to the problem is actually one I have been able to accept. In which case, summarise it, make sure it's agreed, and agree when you will review things.'

'And if it's not acceptable?' queried Sam.

'Ah well,' Gordon grinned, 'then you really have to step up to the mark and show your management credentials. In that case you will have to say why not, propose your solution and ask for agreement to that.'

'I'm with you so far,' said Sam, 'but what happens if you get to this point and they don't agree?'

'Well,' Gordon leaned forward with the air of a poker player about to lay down a winning hand. 'The psychologists, or to be more accurate, the behaviourists, say there is no behaviour change without consequences. So in the final analysis you may just have to spell out that although what you are after is a good agreement...' (Sam rather liked that phrase and made a mental note of it for future use) '...you may have to spell out what the consequences of not reaching a good agreement might actually be.' Sam winced slightly at that.

'And you have had to do that?' he asked.

'Oh, I have always made that absolutely clear,' Gordon replied. 'And that's precisely because it's not personal, it's business. By which I mean that there are a lot of people earning their livelihood here at DecisionMaker, just as there have been in the other businesses I have worked in, and I won't have people who want to be difficult, or behave badly, jeopardise what everyone else is working towards.'

'And how often have you had to stand on an ultimatum like that?' asked Sam.

'Oh I have always stood on the ultimatum,' said Gordon, standing up rather impressively, 'but I have never actually had to carry it out.'

'Sorry?' said Sam, feeling very confused.

'I may just have been very lucky,' said Gordon with a grin, 'but I have always found that people got where I was coming from pretty rapidly and they either decided they wanted to work with me, or they didn't. And don't misunderstand me, Sam, I have never done anything else than pleasantly point out to people that what I expect is that they behave in accordance with the company values and put in a reasonable amount of well-directed effort. That's always worked pretty well for me.'

CHAPTER 13

BUSY BUSY
(Conversation #3: 'How should we be behaving?')

Sam caught up with Jane just after lunch. Not ideal, he thought, but no time like the present. Above all, Sam realised that he had to nip things in the bud. Discontent spreads rapidly, he knew, and even if the attitude itself is not always contagious, it is always upsetting to others nearby. He also wanted to make sure he afforded Jane some privacy, which at DecisionMaker was not always easy. Going outside had been the obvious option for his conversation with Sayeed. Sam guessed that Jane would immediately be uneasy if he suggested going out for coffee – and she might well refuse altogether.

Jane's chosen job title was 'Busy Busy Work Work'. Second oldest in the team after John, she also had a reputation as the most consistent performer. With a high-flying husband in the City and two primary-school-aged children, Jane was a do-it-all, have-it-all kind of person who loved her work and was a regular high achiever. Every business needs to plan how work will be distributed throughout the organisation and Jane was primarily responsible for that planning at DecisionMaker. Always keenly interested in improving efficiency and accuracy, nothing gave Jane more pleasure than being able to map out a process from beginning to end, always with an eye to possible improvements. Jane also enjoyed leading sessions at team meetings such as updates on information from around the company and from outside. Jane also enjoyed leading sessions at team meetings, such as updates on information from around the company and from outside. Jane was popular, Sam knew, and ambitious. Would his promotion cause a problem between them, he wondered? He managed to find one of the mood rooms, areas set up by marketing to represent DecisionMaker's customer profiles. Fortunately, the one representing the working environment of a large corporation was available so they sat down in the nearest thing to a conventional office in the whole DecisionMaker building. Sam was careful to sit on the same side of the large desk as Jane – he was not after pulling rank or being high-handed.

'So what's this about?' Jane started aggressively. Stay calm, Sam reminded himself, and state the problem.

'It's about this morning's meeting,' he said calmly, 'and to be frank, unacceptable behaviour.'

'Unacceptable behaviour!' snorted Jane. 'To who?'

'To me, and actually to the business as a whole. We do have a set of values,' he reminded her, 'and they include "Be positive" as well as "Excellence – set the bar high".'

'And your point exactly?'

'Jane, sitting in a meeting and being negative, saying the subject has nothing to do with you, that's not how we do things around here. You don't need me to tell you that. But I do have to tell you it's not acceptable behaviour. It's not helpful to the business and it's not respectful to the other members of the team.'

Jane said nothing and after a short pause Sam went on.

'So what I am expecting is that we can put this behind us and that I can rely on you to engage with the rest of the team. Even if you think what's under discussion has nothing to do with you, your thoughts and ideas can still be valuable.'

'I just don't understand why I can't be left alone to get on with my job,' Jane muttered.

'Most of the time you can, and that's fine,' Sam confirmed. 'But that doesn't give you permission to disengage or to be unhelpful in meetings.'

There was another pause, during which Sam sneaked a covert glance at the notes he had scribbled down whilst talking to Gordon. 'Ask for their perspective' jumped out at him.

'So what's your view?' he asked, and waited.

'OK, so I was angry,' Jane admitted at last. 'It's not all to do with work, but I don't really want to go there.'

'No need to, let's stick with what we can do at work.'

'I can't seem to get anything done. I can see lots of areas for improvement but everyone is way too busy to listen and they all think what they are doing is OK, even when I can see they are using all kinds of workarounds.'

'OK,' said Sam carefully. 'I can see why that would be frustrating – and shame on me because I didn't know you felt like that. I thought you did a really good job with that analysis of the upload approvals process.'

'Yes, that was quite good, but only because Don Hale liked it.'

'Well, we are also going to have to get other people on board, and Don is pretty useful to have on your side when it comes to implementing a process change like that. I know you said you wanted to be left alone to get on with things, but it doesn't always work like that.'

'I suppose not,' said Jane, less angry now. 'I'm sorry I was angry in the meeting this morning,' she said at last. 'It wasn't good behaviour and I'm not proud of it. What do you want me to do?'

'I'm not after an apology or anything like that! It's more what you think you can do to stop it happening again.'

Jane thought for a moment. 'I guess I need to find a way to leave my baggage at the door when I come in to situations like that.'

'Sounds good. Like going through the airport.'

'Sorry?' asked Jane.

'Well, you have a ticket to the meeting, you are checked in, and all you need to do is go to the Bag Drop and leave everything there except what you need on the flight.'

For the first time Jane smiled. 'I actually like that, you know,' she said, reflecting on it. 'And that's about the first thing in the last forty-eight hours that's actually made me smile. OK, the Bag Drop. I'll remember that.'

'Great,' said Sam, 'and thanks.' He was tempted to ask whether there was anything else he could do but thought better of it. One step at a time, he reminded himself. This was the conversation I wanted to have with Jane, he thought, don't clutter it up with other stuff.

CHAPTER 14

TEENAGE KICKS

'How was *your* day?' Laura asked almost as soon as Sam got through the door that evening, and there was something in that emphasis that made him wary.

'Well, it started out badly but got a little better towards the end,' he began cautiously.

'How so?' asked Laura, who was in the kitchen busy chopping up vegetables.

'The bad start was getting called in by Arnold Kramer and told we have a potentially life-threatening, well, business-threatening, situation with a client.' Laura looked up sharply at that.

'That doesn't sound good,' she said, leaving Sam feeling as though it might be at least partly his fault.

'No, it's not me, nor anyone in my team…' he didn't get any further.

'No, I meant we have a mortgage to pay, household bills, a car on finance and we need two salaries coming in.' Laura banged the knife down on the chopping board. Sam decided to change tack slightly.

'It's going to be all right,' he said, wincing a little inwardly. It wasn't quite a lie, but since he couldn't actually know it was true it felt a bit like one. 'But you asked me about my day, which is great by the way, and thank you. What's been happening with you?'

'It's Emma again.' Laura shook her head and stared down at the chopping board. 'I cannot seem to have any sort of a conversation with her without it turning into a row. She just throws everything back at me. When I was her age I wouldn't have dared to speak to my mother like that. I just don't know what to do about it and I'm fed up with it – and with her!'

'Are we back on tattoos again?'

'No, thank goodness.'

'Then what is it?'

'She tells me she is doing homework and when I look in, to ask her about something completely different, she is on Facebook, or Pinterest, or whatever they are all on these days, clearly not doing her homework, and before I can even say anything she blows up at me about invading her privacy!'

'Do you want me to have a word with her?' Sam asked, not relishing the prospect for a moment.

'No, actually, I don't,' Laura came back. 'It's not going to help if Emma thinks that every time she and I fall out I come running to you. I just want some way of dealing with her that doesn't cause me to get upset.'

If there was one thing Sam had learned during the time he and Laura had been together it was not to rush in too quickly to try to solve a problem. Sometimes, he knew, when people are hurting, and even when they seem to be asking for a solution, what they really want first is comforting.

'I get that completely,' he said, moving round the counter and putting an arm around his wife's shoulder. 'Let's get supper sorted out first and then have a chat about it,' he suggested. Which got a nod, a sniff and a brief 'OK.'

* * * * *

'Just so you know,' Emma announced huffily, marching in to the kitchen, 'I have finished my essay as well as managing to talk to *my friends*, when I'm allowed to.' She sat down and started scrolling on her phone.

Sam caught Laura's eye in a meaningful way. Laura pursed her lips as she started to serve the meal but said nothing. As she put Emma's plate down in front of her, Sam pointed significantly at Emma's phone without saying anything. Emma saw it, and although she gave an exaggerated sigh she closed the phone cover and put it down on the table. After that the meal passed off uneventfully and Emma retreated back to her room while Sam and Laura cleared the dishes away and then sat back down at the table.

'You see?' said Laura, sounding a little helpless. 'Even when she's not on the warpath, she's being sullen, conceited and… and… oh I don't know what else,' she stopped and then added suddenly, 'and you never did get to tell me about you day. Oh, Sam, I'm sorry, I can't seem to do anything right.'

'Don't be daft,' Sam consoled her, 'and my day is not that important by comparison.'

'Tell me anyway. Please.'

So Sam started with the meeting in Dr Kramer's office, playing down the part about the funding round and moving rapidly on to the team meeting and the good thinking that had emerged from that.

'So that was the bit that was a bit better?' Laura asked.

'Well, that was definitely better, but no, the good bit was when I went to check in with Gordon Blaine about Sayeed's idea. Whether Exigenta had actually used our software to make their decision about investing in RRI, and come to that whether anyone at RRI has actually been using DecisionMaker to inform what they do.'

'And the answer?'

'Well, we don't know yet – Gordon hadn't been able to speak to them at that point.'

'So what was so good?'

'Well, Gordon gave me a way to speak to Jane about her being totally negative and really quite disruptive in the team meeting.'

'Which was?'

Sam quickly ran through Gordon's formula for holding a 'difficult' conversation, with Laura looking more and more intrigued. Eventually she said, 'Run that past me again, would you?' and Sam did.

'Just let me make sure I've got this,' said Laura after Sam's repeat. 'You say what the problem is, from your point of view, at least. Then you say why it's a problem – to you, anyway,' Laura added.

'That's right,' Sam confirmed.

'Then you say what you expect.'

'Yep.'

'OK, then the bit I wasn't expecting. You ask for their, what was it? Oh, I know, you ask for their perspective, and then you ask for their solution?'

'You've got it,' Sam nodded.

'And if their solution is OK with you, you check it back, so that you have both got it, and then you agree on it?'

Sam nodded again.

'And if their solution is not acceptable to you, say why not, propose your solution and ask for agreement.'

'I didn't actually have to do that bit with Jane,' Sam said, 'which was a bit of a relief, to be honest.'

'No, but I'm thinking I might have to with Emma,' said Laura, smiling for the first time that evening.

'Hang on a minute,' said Sam, startled. 'Gordon Blaine is a great manager, but I have no idea whether he's a good parent or not. We were only talking about a business conversation.'

'Too bad,' grinned Laura. 'The cat's out of the bag now. And I remember exactly what the last part was. You said: "You may need to be explicit about the consequences of not reaching a good agreement." I think our teenager may have met her match!'

CHAPTER 15

DELEGATION
(Conversation #4: 'Who's really doing this?')

By Thursday, when John returned to work, the DecisionMaker PR effort was in full swing. Gordon had confirmed that Exigenta had indeed invested in RRI before becoming a DecisionMaker customer and in a stroke of genius had persuaded the CEO of Exigenta, a high-flyer named Marcus Cranbourne, to hold a press conference. In return for a period of discount, plus some sweeteners on numbers of licences and renewal extensions, Marcus had publicly taken the line that 'things do go wrong from time to time, even in the best run businesses.' The follow-up was that Exigenta worked ceaselessly to improve every business it was invested in and, in addition to fully investigating the incident at RRI and putting new and stringent security measures in place, they would also be investing further in new and sophisticated technology. There followed a blatant plug for DecisionMaker as a key tool in Exigenta's growth. In return, Gordon negotiated with Sophie Ayar to re-assign her best writer to creating a case study of Exigenta's use of DecisionMaker, carefully leaving out any mention of RRI.

'I really don't know how you managed that,' Sam exclaimed to Gordon as their paths crossed on Thursday morning.

'It's all part of the genius I am paid for here,' returned Gordon with a grin. 'It's just a matter of looking for the win-win. I had a pretty shrewd idea that if I flattered Marcus Cranbourne a little about how brilliant he and everyone else at Exigenta is, and then offered that, on account of them being such an important customer…'

'Which they are, aren't they?' Sam interjected.

'Oh, yes, but you don't usually want to give away a negotiating position by giving anyone the impression they are absolutely vital to your business. Anyway, I sacrificed a little of that in exchange for the idea that we could help their PR effort over RRI, and we could scratch each other's backs a little, and it worked rather well. How did your conversation go?'

'Sorry?' asked Sam, who was still following Gordon's story.

'Your person who wasn't behaving so well in the team meeting.'

'Oh, yes,' Sam nodded thoughtfully. 'Well, we haven't had another meeting yet so I suppose the proof of the pudding will be in the eating, but the conversation itself seemed to go very well. What I mean is that,' he paused, realising he was about to say Jane's name, 'the person concerned came up with their own solution.'

'What was that?'

'To leave your baggage at the door. Before you come into the meeting that is. We came up with the idea of a Bag-Drop, like you have at the airport. You've got your ticket to the meeting, you're checked in, so you drop off your bag – with all your baggage in it – and just take what you need into the meeting.'

'What you need being an open mind and a good attitude, presumably?'

'Pretty much, yes.'

'Good for you, laddie,' said Gordon. 'I'm very pleased that worked for you.'

'Oh, well, actually,' Sam carried on quickly, 'you haven't heard the best bit.'

Gordon cocked his head to one side. 'What's that then?' he asked.

'My wife is about to try it out on our daughter, Emma.'

Gordon whistled, then laughed. 'Well good luck with that. You'd better let me know how that goes as well. If you're still alive to tell the tale!'

They parted and Sam went to find John and fill him in on developments.

* * * * *

John, the Creator of Great Experiences, was around Sam's age, and Sam respected his strong history of achievement in customer service. John was married with two teenage children; he was a solid worker and someone who consistently delivered against his targets. Sam felt very strongly that he could not afford to lose John. He would need to keep him on board.

'Frankly, although I don't enjoy being ill, I think I'm rather glad I missed that,' said John when he had heard Sam out. 'So the Exigenta-RRI thing is OK?'

'Looks like it,' said Sam. 'And I'm very glad you're back. Are you feeling OK?'

'I've felt better. Did something to my back over the weekend. The doctor's given me some strong painkillers and told me to keep moving, so here I am.'

'I'm sympathetic, but I am going to need your help. Exigenta was one thing, we still have to show Dr Kramer that we can do what he's asking.'

'And that you're the man for the job?'

'Well,' Sam paused, slightly thrown by John's remark. 'Did you want the management role?' he asked suddenly.

'Oh, no, that's the last thing I wanted when Kathy left. I thought it was a bit of a poisoned chalice if you want my honest opinion. I'm not saying I don't want more responsibility, but I'm far more interested in the customer-facing bit of what I do than in the internal Ops stuff. If anything, I'd rather go somewhere else and do that.'

'Ah,' said Sam.

'Problem?' asked John.

'Well, only if you decide you want to go,' Sam came back. 'First, that's good to know, thanks for telling me. I think potentially there is a much bigger role here in customer services than we have had in the past and I'm really prepared to push that agenda for you.'

John nodded thoughtfully, giving Sam an appraising glance. 'And in the meantime?' he asked, raising an eyebrow.

'What I need right now is an internal focus,' Sam told him, watching carefully for the reaction.

'You're talking about the deadline at the end of this month then?'

'Yes,' confirmed Sam.

'Well,' John shrugged, 'that's only two weeks away. I can live with something for two weeks. What is it you want?'

Sam took a deep breath. 'I really need to get this right,' he thought.

'You run customer feedback programmes, don't you?' he began.

'Yes, as part of the whole customer services function I get one-to-one feedback from customers, but we also use a simple online tool to dip sample satisfaction.'

'Dip sample?' queried Sam.

'Yes, we don't ask everyone all the time. People can rapidly get fed up with that, so we use a system that is semi-randomised. "Semi" because it makes sure it isn't accidentally asking someone it asked last month, for instance.'

'OK,' Sam acknowledged. 'And what does it ask?'

'Well, again we vary the questions, and we try to make things a bit quirky – we've found that people are more likely to respond if it's not all deadly serious. Actually, our response figures are pretty much industry-leading, so we must be doing something right.'

'Mmm, so here's the thing,' Sam pitched in, 'if we are going to make a difference here, or at least point the way to *how* we could make a difference, I think we should be asking people here for feedback, ideas, suggestions, all of that.'

'Yes, for sure,' John agreed, 'but we already have a staff satisfaction survey, and the results on that are pretty good, aren't they?'

'Yes, they are,' confirmed Sam, 'which tells me that it's not really asking the right questions, or at least not finding out the right things. If everyone was really excited about what we're doing here, and really engaged with what they are doing, we wouldn't be having these problems with missed deadlines, and all the finger-pointing and blame that goes with it. Something's gone wrong.' Sam was warming to his subject now but John returned them to the point.

'What is it you want me to do?' he asked.

'I want you to conduct a very rapid internal survey, but it will need to be exactly what you said, a dip sample, because we don't have time to ask everyone, and I don't want to seem to be running an alternative staff survey, but I need to get an insight, an inside view, of what's going on.'

'And how I do the survey is up to me?'

'Yes. I want enough information to get a good handle on what has gone wrong around here in terms of how people are thinking and behaving.'

'And you want answers by when?'

'By the end of next week. I know that's a stupidly short timescale, but that's how it is.'

John thought for a moment. 'OK,' he said, 'what can't I do?'

'Good question,' said Sam, 'let's see. You can involve anyone else who is willing to be involved; in fact, you can get as much help as you like, but I don't want you to hand the whole project over to someone else. You can't spend anything outside the existing budget. You can approach anyone you like but either as "I" – meaning you of course – or "we", no "Sam's told me to" or "Sam's asked me to." You have my full authority, but I don't want you to go round invoking my name as a higher authority. If you need help just come back to me.'

'Fair enough,' said John after a moment. 'I can see why you say that – it's really annoying when someone comes along telling you they are only asking because their boss has told them to.'

'Good,' said Sam. 'Now just to be really clear, you run it all back past me again.'

John ticked off all the points on his fingers as he went through everything they had agreed.'

'Great, just one more,' added Sam when John had finished. 'Because the timescale is so short I'd like a daily check-in, just so that we both know where we are all the time.'

'No problem, I'll keep you bang up to date,' confirmed John.

* * * * *

The commute home gave Sam a little time for reflection. His conversation with John had gone better than he had expected. OK, so John had been willing, helpful even, and he was experienced, but Sam had seen John be quite difficult with Kathy in the past. He thought back to Kathy's days in charge and his own experiences. It occurred to him that Kathy had often been quite muddled when she had asked team members to do things. The conversation would frequently flit between what she wanted done, and why it was needed. Sometimes there had been confusion over when she was expecting to get things back. By the time he arrived home, Sam thought he had the answer.

'I think I've just successfully delegated something,' he told Laura.

'Isn't that what managers are supposed to do?' she asked a little tartly.

'Well, yes it is, one of the things at least, but I hadn't ever really thought about how to do it before. I just knew it was really important that I got John to agree to do this and to get it done quickly.'

'So what did you do?'

'Well I got it clear in my mind first. Task, timing, limits and a check-back.'

'You are now speaking complete gobbledygook.'

'Sorry, that's my way of remembering it. It would be pretty bad if I found something that worked and promptly forgot how I'd done it.'

'And now I suppose you want to tell me all about it?'

'I just did. I was really clear about what the task was. I mean I told John exactly what the aim was, and why it was important, I described what I needed, I gave him a general outline and enough detail that he could be clear about the result.'

'I can see that might work,' said Laura patiently.

'I set the timescale,' Sam went on without really pausing, 'and, given that it is really urgent, it was crucial to do that, but at the same time I realised that it would always be important to be specific about how long someone has got to deliver something.'

Laura reduced her input to simply nodding.

'Then actually John asked me something really useful – he asked what he could and couldn't do, so it wasn't just "get me the result at any cost." That's the bit I called limitations. I mean there could have been a whole lot more in there, but mostly limits of authority, budget and that seemed to cover it. Then, and this is something I realised after Arnold Kramer called us all in over the Exigenta thing, he just told everyone what he wanted. He didn't check back with anyone that what *they* thought he had asked for was what he actually wanted. So I got John to outline it back to me,' Sam finished triumphantly. 'Ah, sorry,'

DELEGATION

he had looked up to see Laura's blank face and far-away look. 'Hmm, boring. And I haven't asked you about your day,' he trailed off. Laura shook her head.

'No, actually it sounds quite interesting. I have just realised that's what my boss does. Not what you just described, but more like Kathy. He can't seem to delegate anything properly, so he doesn't get what he wants, and then goes back to doing it all himself. Which stresses him, and sends me and the rest of the team home in a foul mood more often than not.'

'Difficult,' said Sam without adding any more.

'What I am wondering,' Laura went on, 'is whether I could sort of do what you were talking about in reverse. If I could make him pin down the task really specifically, make sure of the timescale, check my limits and then told him exactly what I was going to do and by when, he couldn't really complain, could he?'

'I wouldn't have thought so. And after all, if you do that and he says "yes, that's it", then there is a pretty good chance that you will be delivering exactly what he wants, which might brighten up his day.'

'And mine,' said Laura thoughtfully. 'Just because he's rubbish at delegating doesn't mean I have to be rubbish at being delegated to.'

This time it was Sam's turn to say 'Let me know how you get on.'

CHAPTER 16

HEARTS AND MINDS

Tuesday morning came as a reminder of just how urgent things were. Sam's deliberately early arrival at DecisionMaker coincided with Arnold Kramer's.

'Morning, Sam,' Dr Kramer said briskly. 'How's it going?'

Sam rightly divined that a simple 'OK' was not quite going to do it, while at the same time realising Kramer would not have the patience for a detailed account of things while he was heading into the building.

'We've made some really good progress,' he said, trying to sound a lot more confident than he felt, 'got a few more things to sort out, but I'll be back to you before the month is up.'

Kramer turned to face Sam. 'Good. Call Jennie and get something in my diary.' Sam couldn't read anything in his face. 'And make sure it's good, Sam, we need results.'

As Sam checked his email, Slack, texts, and Twitter he was really thinking through what progress he had actually made. It didn't feel like very much. He needed to check in with Rosie and see if she was making progress or having much effect. The same with Sayeed – he might be about to dramatically improve his reporting, but would that really be enough to make the difference Arnold Kramer was looking for? As for Jane, getting her back onside with a good attitude was definitely something of an achievement, provided it was a lasting one, but apart from that he wasn't sure what he would be able to say that would convince Dr Kramer he was delivering business-changing results.

John's project seemed more hopeful. If he could get to the core of what had changed in the business, how the original 'can-do' attitude had started to erode, how 'all for one and one for all' had become 'all someone else's fault', then he might stand a chance. After all, Sam thought, it was a tech business, but, for the time being at least, it was still run by people, and people had hearts and minds.

Which reminded him rather abruptly that he hadn't had a sensible conversation with Debbie. Debbie had joined from another tech company. She had lots of ideas, Sam had noticed, but also had a tendency to talk fondly about how much better things had been in her previous company. Sam knew that Debbie was seen as having high potential, both in her role and more senior roles. He didn't doubt her abilities, but he wondered about her expectations.

In amongst the meetings, requests, calls and emails of the day Sam managed to catch up briefly with Rosie and Sayeed. Both assured him that things were going really well, but he could draw out little hard evidence of real progress. Jane was clearly making an effort to be more positive, although it seemed to Sam that making the effort was costing her quite an effort.

All in all, it was a rather wearing and unproductive day, and Sam was not sorry when he could reasonably leave the office and head home again.

CHAPTER 17

CURFEW

The journey home took longer than usual and Sam was quite late when he turned the key in the front door and stepped in. As he walked into the kitchen he heard a door slam, followed by the sound of footsteps coming rapidly downstairs. Laura marched into the kitchen holding a mobile phone in front of her. One which Sam immediately knew to be Emma's.

'Hi darling,' Sam began lamely, 'everything OK?'

'Shouting, screaming, threats and now sulking,' replied Laura crisply.

'On account of…?' Sam asked more out of politeness than really wanting to know. The last thing he needed was another upset on the home front.

'The digital deadline,' Laura told him. 'I have been talking to Em for weeks about the fact that she gets extremely agitated by all the "he said, she said" debates she and her friends have on their phones every evening, especially approaching bedtime.'

'And you have imposed a curfew?' asked Sam.

'In effect, yes. But I did exactly what you said. I explained what the problem was, what I expected, I asked for Em's solution, which by the way was not acceptable to me…'

'I guess that would be that we leave her alone to do whatever she wants because she is almost grown up now and we have no right to tell her what she can and can't do…'

'Exactly,' confirmed Laura. 'So I gave her my solution, asked for her agreement and outlined the consequences of our not reaching a good agreement.'

'Which is?'

'We have a digital deadline of 9 p.m.'

'It's only 8.15,' Sam pointed out.

'I am making a point,' Laura told him. 'Emma will get her phone back first thing in the morning and it's all hers until 9 p.m. tomorrow. After that, she hands it over until the following morning.'

'Wow,' said Sam, 'will she really do that?'

'Well, I didn't have to fight her for it. There were a lot of tears and a bit of a tirade about our failures as parents, yours as well as mine by the way, but she did hand it over. Which in a funny way,' Laura paused for a moment, 'probably does mean we have done some things right.'

CHAPTER 18

CAREER
(Conversation #5: 'Where are we heading?')

As it turned out, Sam didn't have long to wait for a conversation with Debbie. She came to him.

'I'm a bit hacked off, Sam,' Debbie weighed in straight away, leaving Sam slightly taken aback.

'Oh? Why?' asked Sam. 'Is it something I've done? Or not done?'

'The second one actually. We had this big team meeting, company in crisis and all that. Rosie is running around like where people put their stuff is going to solve everything. You've set John off on a big project to find out what everyone thinks. Sayeed's banging on about how his new style reports are going to change the world, and you haven't asked me to do anything that will be different, add value, or get me noticed.'

'To be honest, Debbie, I thought you were doing a great job, I still do, and I didn't want to interfere with that. Just at the moment we need everything to be running really sweetly – or at least, that's what we are trying to get back to. All the work you've done with Rosie on changing the work environment, talking to HR about employment policies, switching vendors, and improving processes – it's all great stuff. Really I just want you to do more of all of that.'

Debbie shrugged. 'Doesn't sound like the fast-track to me,' she said.

'Sorry?' asked Sam, feeling slightly nonplussed.

'I was brought in on the understanding that good performance at DecisionMaker meant rapid promotion. My performance reviews to date have been excellent, I have been told I am doing a great job. So...?' Debbie raised her arms, palms up, towards Sam in an eloquent gesture that left him slightly startled.

'Um, can I ask who said that to you?' Sam was ninety-nine per cent sure he knew what the answer would be but wanted to play for time.

'Yes. Kathy,' came the brusque answer.

'Yes, that's rather what I thought.'

'Meaning?'

'Meaning I think Kathy sold you something there she couldn't necessarily deliver.'

Debbie rolled her eyes at that. 'So I should be looking elsewhere then?'

'Hang on,' Sam countered quickly, 'I didn't say that. I don't want you going anywhere else. What I meant was that DecisionMaker is a very flat organisation. I mean in Ops at the moment, there's you, me and then Arnold Kramer. Even if Arnold does bring in an Ops Director, that's still only two possible steps.'

'And you're not going anywhere?'

Swallowing the unbidden thought 'not as far as I know' Sam settled instead for: 'Well, I'm not about to hand in my notice. Look, what I'm saying,' he went on after a moment, 'is that it's not as simple as just doing a good job and picking up a promotion. DecisionMaker is flat, but it is also growing fast. So we all need to think differently about our careers.'

For the first time Debbie looked more interested than hostile, although all she actually said was: 'Oh, really?'

'Yes.' Sam was thinking rapidly now. 'Look, my father was an engineer. He qualified, went to work and expected to work for the same firm all his life. That didn't actually happen, and it came as a bit of a shock to him, but how many people here expect to work for DecisionMaker all their lives?'

'So you are thinking of leaving?'

'No, I like it here, even if things are a bit tough at the moment,' he added truthfully. 'But if we achieve the business plan Dr Kramer will take the company public, unless he gets what he thinks is a better offer from a potential buyer – and there are a few of those out there – and either of those things will change the business massively. Not everyone will like that. A lot of people will want to find another start-up. I'm just saying it's a different world.'

'OK, and where does that leave me?'

'Let me go back to my Dad for a minute. For him, promotion did depend on all the things you said. He did a good job and expected to move up, which he did, but only after a while because junior employees were too junior to promote in his day. You had to gain experience, which often meant simply time-serving. Mind you, there was another side to that, as he discovered.'

'Which was?'

'Older employees were too old to be promoted any more. After a certain point you were past it.' Debbie frowned but said nothing. Sam went on. 'He also learned another valuable lesson. In that kind of company, promotion always meant management. So he ended up being a manager, and not an engineer, when what he really liked was engineering.'

'Again, I don't see where this gets me,' said Debbie, sticking to her guns.

'In our world, it's a lot more fluid. You can gain experience by working on different projects, getting seconded to a special assignment, maybe even arranging a job swap with someone. There's a whole raft of things any of us can do outside work to develop ourselves, learn leadership skills, get technical qualifications online, and actually I think our Learning and Development team are pretty good here.'

'It's mostly technical stuff,' responded Debbie.

'True, but we are a tech company, and some of it is more general and would be extremely valuable anywhere.' He paused, then ploughed on. 'Your performance is good, Debbie, and you are obviously very motivated to succeed. But it does sound a bit as though you are expecting the company to pick up your career so that you are carried along on a wave of success.'

'Well how else does it happen?' Debbie asked, angry again. 'I work very hard here, Sam, you know that. I get along with people, I don't stir things up, and what's my reward?'

Fighting the temptation to reply 'well, you're still here,' Sam said instead: 'I think you can be exceptionally well rewarded here, Debbie, but you may have to think a little differently.'

'OK, so what do you suggest?'

Sam took a deep breath. 'First of all you probably need to get a little more exposure to Dr Kramer, and to Dale Howson. I'd cultivate Sophie as well, learn a bit more about how the other parts of the business function. I'd try to find a mentor, or a sponsor. It won't be Arnold, but maybe one of the others, or someone else on the board. Expand your networks, outside as well as inside the company, and I'm not suggesting you go and look for another job, it's just that the people I know who are most successful always seem to be the best networked – they always know who to ask or who to go to about anything. And look for opportunities. I know you work very hard, but maybe you are a bit too head-down in your current role.'

'Can't see the wood for the trees, you mean?'

'I hadn't thought of it like that, but yes, exactly that.'

Debbie looked thoughtful. 'OK, anything else?' she asked.

'Well, how much career planning have you done?'

'Oh come on Sam, how can anyone plan anything these days? You know, change is the only constant and all that. We're all so flexible and agile and I don't know what, we are tying ourselves in knots.'

'I meant more about where you want to end up,' Sam took a conciliatory tone. 'It's true, none of us may know exactly how we are going to get there, but the sort of role, the type of work, that sort of thing is important. It's knowing what you want to get out of it that's important, what really gives you satisfaction.'

'And how about you? Is this all part of your plan?'

'Well, in a funny way it is. I never set out wanting to be a manager. But I would like to run something of my own one day. And it had occurred to me that if that venture were to come off, and it was going to be more than just me, I would need to learn how to manage other people, how to create a good team, how to get the best out of everyone. So although it came as a bit of a bombshell, Dr Kramer has done me a huge favour. I would have needed to get this experience somehow.'

'So why not go out on your own now?'

'Oh I'm nowhere near ready yet,' laughed Sam. 'There's a lot I need to learn. About managing people, for a start!'

'You're not doing so badly, you know.' Debbie smiled for the first time in the entire conversation. 'You're the only boss I have had so far that has made me really think about all this. You are basically saying it's up to me, aren't you, rather than up to the company?'

'Well, yes, I think I am. But I am also saying that in my, admittedly rather limited, experience, people who systematically plan their careers tend to not only be more successful, but also to feel much more positive about their careers than those who don't.'

'So in summary?' asked Debbie.

'Well now you are putting me on my mettle, but I would say, fortify yourself with knowledge, learn as much as you can about every aspect of the business, and other businesses, not just about the job you are doing.' Debbie nodded. Sam went on. 'Broaden your experience wherever you can and look for new responsibilities. Keep on asking for feedback, and finally confront yourself.' Debbie looked startled at that. 'What I mean,' Sam reassured her, 'is work out what you really are good at, accept that we all have limitations, be honest with yourself about what you really want, and hear what other people say.'

'Wow,' said Debbie. 'Thought for the day. You have made me think though. One thing you haven't said though is something I was told at BlastOff, where I used to work.' Sam braced himself for another story about how great everything had been at BlastOff but Debbie said something else instead.

'There was a bit of a mantra there: Find out what your boss really wants – and do that.'

'Well maybe, but it sounds a bit cynical to me,' remarked Sam.

'Maybe,' said Debbie, 'but I'm asking anyway. What do you want me to do, Sam? What's really going to help right now?' At which Sam had to laugh.

'That's a good question. And the truth is I'm not sure what the answer is just at the moment.'

'Well, what's top of your agenda? What do you really need?'

'What I really need is something fantastic to present to Arnold by the end of next week. And right now I don't know what that's going to be.'

Debbie thought hard for a moment and then said: 'Why you? I mean, you just said that I should get more exposure at that level, and it's not just me. How about you take the whole team in, and we each present our own bit. That would be more impressive, wouldn't it? It would show that we are all working together to solve the issues – and it would show what a good job you have done to pull the team together.'

'Well,' Sam began slowly, 'that's a great idea, but I'm not sure everyone would be up for it. Arnold can be pretty scathing if he doesn't like what someone is saying, and I don't know how used to presenting people are, especially at that level.'

'Leave that to me. I used to do regular Board and Stakeholder presentations at BlastOff. I can give the others some tips.'

'OK,' Sam said, 'I wonder if we can get Learning and Development involved.'

'What will they do?'

'They were running some short courses on presentation skills a while ago. I'll see if we can get a half-day training on it. That would give everyone a bit of practice first, plus, as you say, some tips and technique.'

'All right, but you are happy for me to go round the team and sell everyone on the idea?'

'I thought that would be my job?'

'I am creating opportunity and accepting responsibility,' Debbie replied with a smile. 'You can thank me later. I'll thank you now by the way. Great career conversation, Sam. Thanks very much.' Then she was gone.

CHAPTER 19

PREPARATION

Sam was on his way to Learning and Development when he ran into Zoe Brookes, DecisionMaker's Head of HR.

'Hi, Sam, how are you doing?' Zoe asked.

'Good, thanks,' replied Sam. 'I was just looking for Eva. Is she around?'

'I saw her not long ago, she's around somewhere, but just before you go – I'm glad I caught you.'

'Oh?'

'I was chatting to Chris Cullen just now. Apparently Chris didn't have an appraisal meeting with Kathy last year. Kathy postponed it a couple of times and then it never happened. I've checked and there's nothing on the system. So that needs putting right – and more importantly, Chris said she wanted to sit down with you. So there you go, open door. It'll be your first as a manager here, won't it?'

'Yes, it will,' admitted Sam.

'Well let me know how you get on,' said Zoe brightly, before adding, 'must dash, recruitment interviews this afternoon.'

Sam found Eva Nowak and explained what he wanted.

'You won't want to take everyone out for a day then, will you?' was Eva's first response.

'Or even half a day if we can do something in less.'

Eva pursed her lips. 'Well, OK. I have an idea. If we can get everyone well briefed beforehand, then I could spend two hours with the team on Wednesday next week before you go into the presentation on Friday. That's close enough that everyone will remember things, but far enough away for them to make some adjustments and practice a bit more before presenting for real. You know that's the most important thing? Practice out loud what you are going to say, as though your audience is right there in front of you.'

'You mean literally say it out loud?'

'Exactly,' said Eva emphatically. 'It really is the only way.'

'Do you do that?' he asked, surprised.

'Oh yes,' Eva laughed. 'I tell my boyfriend I will be practicing so he does not think I am completely mad, and then I practice. Out loud, in the kitchen, while he is in the other room watching television.'

'Well, I never heard that before.'

'Here is what I propose,' said Eva briskly. 'I will send you some notes on making powerful presentations. They are the notes from the course we developed last year. Back then we had some help from a specialist, now you have just me, but never mind. You give the notes to your team. Using the notes, they should each prepare what they are going to say. You can check the content with everyone but leave how they are going to say it to them – and to me a little bit. Everyone prepares…'

'And everyone practices?' guessed Sam.

'Exactly. Out loud. Then when we all get together next week, it will be practice in front of each other, get feedback, we will fine tune, and by Friday you will have a great set of presentations.'

'I think we'll need them,' said Sam.

'Don't worry. It will be good. That is what we are here for.'

CHAPTER 20

APPRAISAL
(Conversation #6: 'How are we doing?')

Walking away, Sam suddenly thought that he could have asked if Eva had any training notes on how to run a brilliant performance appraisal. He almost turned and went back, but having asked for help with the team presentation he felt slightly embarrassed to ask about something else. His appraisals with Kathy had pretty much been a box-ticking exercise. He wasn't surprised that Kathy had skipped doing Chris's appraisal, he had always had the feeling that Kathy didn't look forward to those meetings and was keen to get them over with as quickly as possible. Then it struck him. 'I'll bet she felt just like I do! Nobody's told me how to do this, I'm not feeling very confident about it. Technically, all I have to do is make an appraisal of how Chris has done against her objectives, get her agreement to that and input the results into the HR system.' Was that really being a good manager, he wondered? It felt a bit like Debbie's career conversation. Chris probably wanted a real conversation about how she was doing. He owed it to her to give it his best shot. But what would that look like?

Sam thought back to previous appraisals before he had joined DecisionMaker. The one he remembered best had been a complete disaster. He had been keen to impress and to get a really good performance rating, so when his manager had opened up with: 'So, how do you think it's gone?' Sam laid it on thick about his achievements, and what had probably started out as a wafer-thin difference between Sam's estimate of his own performance and his manager's view had widened into a great abyss, into which they both fell. By the time his manager had called a halt, suggesting they both calm down, think again and meet a week later, tempers had been running high, with suggestions of expectations unmet, promises broken, moving goalposts, objectives made redundant or impossible by changes in direction or strategy, and a host of other grievances emerging on both sides. Nevertheless, Sam thought, he did want to hear Chris's view of things. The question was, how to do that?

In the end Sam decided that he needed to take charge of the conversation from the outset. So he would start by recognising something Chris was doing well. Not piling on the praise, but just with a simple piece of recognition for a positive beginning. Then he would ask for Chris's view. Thinking about it further, he decided that if he was Chris, he would want to be listened to. He wouldn't want to have to debate everything he said point by point. Much better he thought to suspend his judgement, take some good notes and hear Chris out. In fact, he decided, at that point he would ask Chris what she thought hadn't gone so well, and what she might want to improve or develop, before he offered any commentary. Only at that point, he decided, would he start to ask for things he wanted Chris to do or to change. By then, he reasoned, they stood the best possible chance of being on the same page, and if Chris was willing to talk about change and development then he could use the same approach he had taken with Rosie. The Coaching Conversation, as he now thought of it. Finally, he thought, he needed to avoid going back into praising what Chris had done well in the past. He wanted them both to be looking forwards. What he needed to do was build Chris's confidence so that she could do what was being asked of her and keep the focus on the future.

By now Sam's notepad was covered in rather random jottings so he took a clean sheet and wrote down the following words:

Recognise

Empathise

Encourage

Ask

Coach

Build

It didn't make a snappy acronym: REEACB didn't exactly trip off the tongue, although if he put 'and' in between REE and ACB it did fit the tune of the Aretha Franklin song 'Respect'. He rather liked that, respect was important, and with that in mind, he realised, he needed to find a good time to have the conversation with Chris, he didn't end up postponing the meeting, ensure they were both properly prepared for it, and make sure it would be in a comfortable place but one where they could have an open conversation.

He managed to book the larger of DecisionMaker's two meeting rooms, the one with windows and some natural light, and fend off the efforts of Marketing who claimed they desperately needed it at exactly the time Sam had booked. He had a brief chat with Chris ahead of time to ask her to prepare, and suggested that as well as reviewing her objectives she might have a more general think about areas in which she felt strong and those where some development might help. He added that Chris might also think about areas she saw as opportunities, and things that were frustrating her. In the meantime Sam set about working out what he thought their DecisionMaker DaVinci should be achieving for the business, and what he really wanted and needed from Chris going forward.

* * * * *

'I wanted to start by saying that was a great point you made at the team meeting,' Sam began, 'about whether Exigenta used our software on their investment decisions, or only in the businesses they are invested in.'

'Well, it just suddenly occurred to me,' said Chris. 'Certainly in our meeting nobody knew the answer to that so we were starting to discuss things without really knowing the first thing about the situation.'

'Not very clever, given the business we are in,' agreed Sam with a wry smile. 'Well done for bringing us all back on track.' Chris smiled briefly at that and nodded.

'I'd like to start off by getting your view of things. Hopefully you've had a bit of time to think about that since we spoke?'

'Yes, I have,' Chris responded. 'To be honest, I didn't really have a very clear set of objectives. Kathy rather left it up to me so I sort of outlined some things I thought would be good and she agreed to them.'

'Go on,' said Sam, inwardly acknowledging that it would be difficult to give Chris meaningful feedback against a loose set of objectives, and simultaneously reminding himself to shut up and let Chris tell it her way.

'Well, the big project has been the MPE tool. We have been developing a new part of the system where you input all the information you are applying to the decision you want to make that's come from previous experience. Then the software maps that on to all the different aspects of the current decisions and tells you whether you are being informed – because the situations are similar – or misled because actually they are not the same. Hence MPE – Misleading

Previous Experience. It's a major factor in some really bad business decisions.'

Chris went on to outline at some length her contributions to the project while Sam made notes, and at the end he asked Chris about other things she had been working on. After half an hour Sam had a lot of notes and Chris was looking at him rather expectantly.

'You haven't said anything,' she said curiously.

Sam smiled. 'Well, no. I wanted to hear it from you. Let me check I have understood everything…' And, using his notes, Sam played back what Chris had said. At the end she nodded vigorously and said: 'Yup, that's a pretty good summary.'

'So,' asked Sam, 'is there anything you think you could have done better, or should improve going forwards?'

Chris looked thoughtful. She knew her normal reaction would have been a rather cocky one, that everything was great and she just needed to do more of it, but hearing Sam summarise accurately everything she had just said had made her think.

'I could have been much clearer in my objectives. I thought at the time that if Kathy wasn't going to pin me down, that would give me a lot of wiggle room. Actually, I've just realised it's made it much harder for me to show you what I have been doing.'

'True,' agreed Sam.

'And I've also realised that I hadn't really thought about any development – only about the job I was actually doing.'

'OK, well those are things we can look at together. I've got one for you though.'

'Oh?' Chris looked interested.

'I am wondering whether there is anything in product development that we could use to really hook Arnold Kramer's attention next week. Is there anything at all we could pull out of the hat?'

Chris thought hard and fought back the temptation to say 'I'm working like mad here – what do you want, blood?' Sam's approach had made her feel appreciated. He really had listened, and had shown her that he had a good grasp of what she had been working on, including some of the problems and challenges she had mentioned. She couldn't help but think he deserved something back for that.

'There is one thing,' she began cautiously. 'We have been working on another Risk Assessment Tool. If we brought that forward, or at least brought the projected launch date forward, we could play off the RRI thing. I mean you wouldn't use that exact example because it's too close to home, but we could point up some instances from other places and be able to say: "that couldn't happen again with our new product".'

'Well that would be great! I know Arnold is on the warpath about missed deadlines so if we can help pull something forward that is definitely a quick win.'

'It would be a bit of good news as well. I think a lot of the issue here at the moment is that we always used to focus on the positives and take a positive view of problems, but we seem to have stopped celebrating all the good stuff, all the things we do well, and everyone focusses too intently on any little thing that goes wrong.'

'You know you're absolutely right, Chris!' Sam sat up suddenly. 'This isn't really to do with your appraisal – except that I am going to give you a "Game Changer" rating for that.'

Chris looked startled. 'I was expecting something pretty mid-division.'

'Better than that for what you have been doing. "Plus One" for pitching in with the Risk Assessment Tool piece, but "Game Changer" for what you've just said!'

'Well, I'm still not sure how.'

'I'll come to that. First, let's get down to how you are going to set some clearer objectives, bring the Risk Assessment Tool forward and keep the MPE project on track with the product development team. So, let's take the first one first, what would a good goal be there do you think?'

And with that Sam slipped effortlessly back into what had worked so well with Rosie – the Coaching Conversation. An hour later they had covered all of the topics and Sam ended by picking up on some of what Chris had said in terms of her past accomplishments – and how she had achieved them – to build her confidence about succeeding with her new goals.

'Thanks, Sam,' said Chris as they left the meeting room. 'That was really helpful. You have still got me around the Game Changer idea, though. Come on – what was that all about?'

'I'm going to keep my powder dry on that one,' Sam replied with a grin, 'but you won't have long to wait. I'm calling a team meeting for tomorrow – and all will be revealed.'

In the remainder of the day Sam talked to everyone in the team individually. 'A bit of an ask I know, but if I'm buying, could we all meet at the Treacle Factory half an hour before coming in to work tomorrow?' The Treacle Factory was a coffee bar by day and a cocktail bar by night. It was housed in a building on the site of what had once been a treacle factory and was very popular, even given the level of competition it faced locally. As well as good coffee, Sam knew they served a large variety of herbal teas, loose-leaf teas, brewed lattes, and even bubble teas. Something for everyone.

CHAPTER 21

CONSIDERATION

Eight o'clock the next morning saw Sam's team clustered around a rather too small table with a variety of drinks, from coffees and teas to green smoothies and juices, and an equally eclectic variety of things to eat.

'I hope I'm right in saying we are all preparing presentations for our session with Eva next week?' Sam started off. Everyone affirmed this with a nod or a quiet 'yes'. 'Right,' Sam went on, 'well done. If we all go into that session as well prepared as we can be we will get the most out of it – and be as well set-up as we possibly can be for Dr Kramer on Friday morning. Now, here is what I propose. On Thursday evening we take over the downstairs room at NightOwls. I will scrounge up a bit of budget to put behind the bar and kick things off, and we invite the rest of the business to a celebration.'

'Of what?' asked Rosie.

'Well, that's just the point. The price of entry is going to be "come with something to celebrate." We'll have an open mic and ask people to get up and say what's great about DecisionMaker, everything we want to celebrate about the business and about working here, and generally remind each other about all the good stuff.'

'I think I see where you are going here,' Debbie chipped in. 'Thursday night's feelgood carries over into the office on Friday.'

'Provided everybody isn't *totally* wasted!' laughed Sayeed.

'Well, yes,' Sam admitted, 'that would rather defeat the purpose. But I'm only talking about a couple of hours after work. I guess a few people might make a night of it, but most people will have a good time and then head on home.'

'We could quietly spread the idea of carrying the party atmosphere back to work in the morning,' suggested Chris.

'I'm certainly in favour of getting back to putting a bit more fun into the day,' agreed John. 'That has been lacking a lot recently. I hadn't really thought about it until you mentioned this, but we always used to celebrate success and more recently we have stopped doing it.'

'That's the thing,' Sam came back in, 'we need everyone to share their successes. We need to build a bit of excitement, get people confident, and optimistic about the future.'

'How about a bit of music?' asked Sayeed, 'Get a bit of a club atmosphere going?'

'Maybe to finish off,' said Sam, 'but I want to keep the focus on this kind of karaoke-success idea – get a real rotation of people coming up to talk about all the good stuff.'

'And how are you going to get people coming up with all these tales of good stuff?' asked Debbie.

'Well,' said Sam with a grin, 'that's where I think we will all need to lead the way. We'll all have prepared our presentations for Dr Kramer. Obviously we are not going to start presenting as such on the evening, but if we each worked out a headline – or a short message…'

'Like an elevator pitch?' Jane chipped in.

'That kind of thing,' Sam agreed. 'Probably a bit more than just a one liner – although, on reflection a really good one-liner would probably do it.'

'Could we do a bit of work on those during the session with Eva?' asked John. 'Coming up with inspirational one-liners is not really my thing, but I'm up for delivering one if I can get a bit of help putting it together.'

'Good idea,' said Sam. 'I'll have a word with Eva so that she knows we all want a headline version of our presentations, and we can try those out on each other as well.'

The breakfast meeting ended cheerfully enough. Sam was settling the bill at the counter when Jane came up.

'Could I have five minutes before we head into the office?' she asked.

'Of course,' said Sam, slightly startled. They sat back down again.

'I've just been noticing,' Jane was looking down at her hands as she spoke, 'well, it's just that you seem to have a real knack for getting on with everyone in the team.'

'I don't know about that!'

'Oh you do. Everyone's just agreed with you that we will all stand up in front of Dr Kramer, now you've got everyone keen on this karaoke celebration thing, and everyone seems really happy.'

'So?'

'Except me of course! I still feel like I'm on the outside of everything.'

'Is that something I've done?'

'No, not at all. It's the opposite really. I just seem to get impatient with people all the time. You listen. I've noticed that about you.' Taking his cue, Sam said nothing. 'How does that work?'

'It wasn't always like this. I used to just wait my turn to talk. After a while – a very long while actually – I realised that if I made the effort to listen then I understood people better. Then I didn't get so impatient, or just think they were being stupid, or whatever it was.'

Jane gave a big sigh. 'I'm having some relationship troubles,' she said. 'That's the "outside work" bit I didn't want to talk about when you pulled me up for being a, well, you know what, in the team meeting.'

'So why now?'

'Because I want to understand how to make things better – at work and at home.'

'Honestly, Jane, I'm not qualified to talk about relationships. I mean, you say I listen, but I think you would get a very different view of that from my wife, Laura. Although I do try,' he admitted ruefully.

Jane said nothing. Feeling completely out of his depth, Sam made a stab in the dark.

'Is it boyfriend trouble?'

'Girlfriend actually,' Jane told him, looking up, 'but I suppose the principle's the same.'

'I'm really not sure I am the best person for you to be talking to about this,' Sam was about to duck out altogether when he saw the look on Jane's face. 'There is one thing, though...' Worryingly, Jane's face lit up at that. 'I'm just thinking that you do work very hard. You put in a lot of hours and you are quite intense about what you do.'

'That's what Ellie says,' responded Jane, looking almost wistful.

'Look, I really don't know, and I am out of my depth here,' honesty is the best policy, thought Sam, 'but if you took a couple of days off, I mean, yes we are being pushed at the moment, and pushed hard, but if you took Friday and Monday off and had a long weekend, maybe go away somewhere with Ellie, then you could forget about work for a few hours somewhere in the middle of that and have a chance to talk properly.'

'I think I need to listen, not talk.'

'Well maybe, but you know what I mean.'

'Would that really be OK?' Jane asked.

'It's OK by me,' said Sam, 'and I would lay money that you are owed holiday.'

Jane nodded. Then she stood up suddenly, looked Sam in the eye and said: 'Thank you, Sam,' adding, 'I really mean that,' before grabbing her bag and heading for the door.

CHAPTER 22

SHORT WEEKEND

A long weekend. That was a very appealing idea, but not to be for Sam. Something lodged in his mind from his conversation with Jane though. He had been a bit absent recently. Perhaps he should do something to make up for that. He broached the subject with Laura over supper.

'I've got another big week coming up next week,' he started.

'Tell me about it,' Laura responded quickly. 'When do you not have?'

'Well, I am hoping that if our presentations to Arnold Kramer hit the mark then the spotlight may be off us for a little while and on someone else.'

'That would be nice. We might get to see something of you.'

'I have been thinking about that. I thought we might go out and do something this weekend.'

'Like what?'

'Well, I hadn't got that far. I was thinking as a family though. What could we do that would include Em?'

'You'll be lucky!' Laura snorted. 'She's still smarting over the digital curfew. I thought that was a bit of a victory at the time but now I'm beginning to wonder.'

'There must be something,' said Sam.

'A trip to the Apple Store?'

'Come on, Laura, it's not like you to be so cynical.'

'I call it realism.'

'Maybe. But a cynic is a passionate person who doesn't want to be disappointed again, and I think that sounds like you.'

Laura paused for a moment, then said: 'Wow. Who said that?'

'I can't remember,' Sam told her honestly. 'I'll look it up and tell you later.'

'Well, I'm certainly not feeling very passionate about motherhood. I can vouch for that.'

'Then we ought to do something about that.' Sam paused. 'I'm no psychologist but I wonder if in attempting to break away and become her own person Em is actually missing you a bit.' Laura said nothing. 'Let's see what we can come up with,' said Sam, and left it at that.

* * * * *

They were getting ready for bed when Laura said: 'I have had a thought. What you said about Em. It would be good if we could get her to come out with us and do something as a family.'

'Great, but we still need an idea of something she might agree to.'

'I've been thinking about that too. She does like Camden Market. I know she goes there with friends sometimes, so provided she doesn't think it's *totally* uncool to go with her parents that might be a possibility.'

'Terrific idea,' enthused Sam. 'We can play ten for a tenner.'

'What's that?'

'You each get to choose ten things that cost ten pounds – or less…'

'That's going to be expensive,' Laura put in.

'Ah well, there is a catch. You make a list as you go round, then you have to choose just one thing from your list that you are actually going to buy. Or in this case that we are going to buy Emma.'

'OK, do I get to play too?'

'Oh we all get to play, it's more fun that way,' grinned Sam. 'I had an idea too. Em likes theme parks, doesn't she?'

'Ye-es,' said Laura warily, 'but I am not going riding rollercoasters if that's what you are thinking.'

'No, Harry Potter was what I had in mind.'

'Really?'

'Yes, the studio tour. We could do the market in the morning and go on from there on the train.'

'I think that might just work. How did you come up with that?'

'Information search,' laughed Sam. 'While you were watching that show I can't stand on television, I emailed a couple of people who have children about Em's age. Theme parks got a big vote. Harry Potter was my idea. Well, with a bit of help from Google.'

* * * * *

'For real?' asked Emma as Sam explained the joys of playing ten for a tenner. Harry Potter clinched it though.

The market was busy, lively and fun. Emma's choice at the end of the game was a set of interlocking multi-coloured bangles which clattered on her wrist and caught the eye. Laura chose a cushion with a picture of a dog wearing a sweater, glasses and a scarf, which she claimed looked just like Sam in one of his 'thoughtful moods'. Sam lingered over a poster of David Bowie in his Ziggy Stardust era superimposed over the music to 'Life on Mars,' but in the end chose a Japanese manga comic about business strategy, though with the text in English.

'Bor-ring!' was Emma's response when he showed it to her.

'Intriguing, to me at least,' Sam grinned. 'Keep an open mind, Em. In your lifetime it's more than likely you will have a job that doesn't exist yet.' Emma threw him a look and Sam added mischievously, 'or you might live in a world in which nobody works.'

'Oh yeah? How would that happen?'

'All the robots would be designed by computers and built by other robots.'

'You're weirder than Harry Potter,' sighed Emma.

'Speaking of which,' said Sam, 'Platform Nine and Three-Quarters beckons.'

* * * * *

They finished the day with an amicable agreement on where to eat, finding somewhere that would provide a meal Emma was happy to photograph and post online to her friends, whilst also offering some choices more to Sam and Laura's taste.

'So, good day out?' Sam asked as they tucked in.

'Actually, yes,' said Emma after a pause.

'Well, I wanted to say that I'm sorry I haven't been around so much this last little while,' Sam went on. 'I felt I needed to give a lot of attention to work, and perhaps I got that a bit wrong.' There was a long pause and then Emma spoke, but to Laura, not to Sam.

'I'm sorry, Mum. I have been a bit out of order lately, haven't I? It all just seemed a bit fraught. I thought you two weren't getting along so well and, well, I just, I just…' she tailed off and then started again. 'Well, I don't really know.' Laura smiled, Sam said nothing but thought, 'that was a conversation I wasn't expecting to hear.'

CHAPTER 23

PRACTICE

Eva's presentation skills workshop started bang on time – and kicked off with a bang. She simply asked someone to stand up and give their presentation in front of the group. There was a short pause and then John said 'All right, I'll give it a go,' and they were off. Although just as John was getting up Eva gave some instructions to the rest of the team.

'You all know what a great presentation sounds like,' she told them, 'and I am sure you have all heard some really terrible ones! The really good ones always command your attention and interest. That may be through a personal story, or by great use of technology, but it probably includes some sort of visual aids, good use of gestures, a lively voice, and maybe a little bit of appropriate humour.' She went on, 'analogies are really helpful if they connect people to your content. Above all, you need to keep up momentum. We listen much faster than we can talk, if you see what I mean, so make sure you project your core message vividly – and with vitality.' Eva looked around. 'So that's what we all want to hear. Please listen to each other and then don't give feedback.' She paused while that registered, leading to puzzled expressions.

'Feed forward instead! When John has given us his presentation I am going to ask all of you to rate it from one to ten. One is you were so bored you fell asleep. Ten is "I tingled all over"! Then you are going to tell John one thing that would make it better next time. So you might say: "Seven, and what would make it an eight would be a bit more passion about why you want it to work".'

With that, they were off, starting with John's presentation about the results so far of his survey. When everyone had given John their rapid-fire thoughts about what would make his presentation better next time Eva asked how he felt about everything everyone had said.

'Brilliant,' said John. 'That was really helpful. In fact, can I do it again and try to incorporate all of that?'

'In a few minutes,' Eva said with a grin. 'We are going to go round and have everyone's first effort and then we will all go again.'

Sam let a couple of the team have their turn before jumping in, he deliberately didn't want to wait until last. His 'feed-forward' was capped by Sayeed with a highly accurate impersonation of Arnold Kramer saying: 'That's all very well, Sam, but what you need to do is…' It was so good that Sam, startled, looked straight at the door, igniting a wave of laughter around the group. 'Got me there,' he had to admit, now grinning himself. 'And?' he asked Sayeed.

'Oh, nine,' said Sayeed, smiling back, 'and what will make that a ten is all of us giving a great presentation on the day.'

'It's going well so far,' Eva told him. 'Who's up next?'

Last to go was Jane, who didn't look too comfortable. Almost as soon as she started though the atmosphere was electric.

'When I joined DecisionMaker,' she began, 'I thought it was *the* place to be. I was *so* enthusiastic I couldn't do enough. All the hours God sends – and a few more. And I *loved* it!' As she said that she put her right hand over her heart and then flung it out wide, as though she were throwing that love out across her audience.

'And we were being *so* successful,' Jane placed the emphasis on certain words very carefully, not overdoing it, just underlining things as she went along. 'But gradually, so gradually I didn't even notice at first,' she made a rippling gesture with the fingers of her right hand, miming a pianist making a long run up the keyboard, 'things started to go wrong.' She paused and looked around. Chris was the first person she made eye contact with and so she spoke directly to Chris. 'So naturally, I tried harder. More hours, more effort. And you know what?' Jane unlocked from Chris and looked around her audience as if she wanted an answer from them, 'things got worse.' She shrugged and pulled a face.

'That,' she went on with heavy emphasis, 'went on for a long time. In fact, it went on until just very recently. To the point where my relationship was on the rocks, where I didn't want to talk to my friends outside work. I most certainly did not want to talk to my mother, who kept calling me up, and I was pretty close to walking out on everything.'

By now even Eva was slightly open-mouthed. This was meant to be a couple of hours on presentation skills, not a group therapy session. She glanced over at Sam, it was his team after all, but he was staring at Jane, who carried on.

'So what happened?' Jane asked suddenly, very loudly and throwing her arms out wide. 'What happened to change all that? To make me feel the way I used to about being here? To make me go back to feeling really positive – and, by the way, probably to have put my life outside work back on track?'

Jane paused. The room was still. It almost seemed as if the world outside had stopped. Then she smiled, a broad, beaming smile, and she shrugged, holding her hands out, palms up.

'I got a *brilliant* manager!' she said triumphantly. 'I got a manager who listened to me, who seemed to care about me and who seemed to be on my side. Yes he read me the riot act about my bad behaviour, but I did need that, and once we got that out of the way, well...'

Jane stopped, to a stunned silence. After what seemed like an age Debbie said 'Ten,' very decisively.

'I'll say so,' said John quietly, 'ten.' Ten followed ten, until finally Sayeed jumped up from his chair shouting, 'What is wrong with you all. Ten is not enough – Jane you are eleven!' At which point Jane walked over from the front of the room, gave Sayeed a big hug, and sat back down in her chair.

* * * * *

'Are you really going to say that on Friday?' Sam asked Jane as the session broke up.

'Well,' Jane turned to look at him, 'I won't if you don't want me to?'

'No, honestly. It's a bit embarrassing personally, that's all. I won't know where to look.'

'Well you can either look at me, or you can look at Dr Kramer and see what he thinks, but if he is half as intelligent as he is made out to be, he should get the message, shouldn't he?'

'What, that I'm great? Or I have bribed you?'

'No, don't be silly, Sam. It's all about how you treat people at work. That's the message. Everyone should have a brilliant manager – that's the point! Let's be honest. We all chose to come out to work. Of course most people pretend it's a duty or an obligation – I have a mortgage to pay, I'm a parent or whatever it may be, but it's still really a choice. Some people end up on the streets, some parents abandon their children. So when we make that choice, to come to work, we deserve to have a brilliant manager.' Sam looked slightly startled. 'And thanks for being one. By the way, I have just made up my mind, I am going to say all that on Friday – whether you like it or not!'

CHAPTER 24

CELEBRATION-KARAOKE

NightOwls was a trendy bar just a few hundred yards from the DecisionMaker offices and was a popular spot. The offer of a free first drink was enough to tempt quite a few people along, and their ranks were swelled by those made curious by the buzz Sam's team had managed to create around their celebration-karaoke. A lot of hints had been dropped about having something to celebrate, without anyone saying what it was.

The main bar area at NightOwls was smart with a lot of mirrors, primary-coloured leather and street art on the walls. Downstairs was more shabby-chic, with mismatched tables and chairs, sections of variously patterned wallpaper separated by scratched wooden panels, and most of the contents of an old ironmongers shop spread about on shelves and in cubby holes. Not Sam's sort of thing at all, but the offer of around fifty people coming in at six o'clock for a drink or two had been enough to secure the space and the use of a microphone for an hour.

At her own request Rosie was first up.

'We've told you all we have something to celebrate,' she said with a big smile, 'and we do. What we are here to celebrate is all the things we all do well, and all the things we like about each other and about working together. Might sound a bit corny, I know, but we realised in our team that we had started focussing on everything that was wrong and we were forgetting to look at all the good things. So I'm standing up to celebrate the fact that we've noticed that – and we are doing something about it.'

Chris followed Rosie up to the mic. 'I'm here to celebrate the fact that I had a great appraisal meeting.'

'You are joking, surely?' called someone from the audience.

'No, I'm not, actually. Thanks, Sam!' said Chris, pointing right at Sam. 'Who's next?' she asked. To Sam's surprise, Art Hopkins, his opposite number in Finance, took the microphone.

'I must find out how you did that, Sam!' he said with a grin and a nod. 'I'm here to celebrate the fact that I have a great team too. I strongly suspect that they all hate our appraisal meetings, sorry about that,' he added to a ripple of laughter, 'but, yes, great team, and DecisionMaker is still a great company.'

After that the mood took hold. While some people were content just to have a drink and chat, a steady stream of people got up to say what they wanted to celebrate. Eventually it became a contest among a small number to name ever more outlandish things, but that just added to the atmosphere. As the party broke up, the buzz in the room was palpable.

CHAPTER 25

DRAGON'S DEN

Arnold Kramer had been surprised, and had seemed a little put out, by Sam's request that they meet in the larger meeting room and that Sam wanted his team to be present.

'I was expecting you to come back and report to me personally,' he had said sharply.

'And I definitely will,' confirmed Sam, 'but the team has worked very hard this month and people deserve credit for what they have done.'

'Very well,' Dr Kramer had said. He hadn't added 'on your own head be it,' but the words seemed to hang in the air.

On Friday morning the team quickly went through their running order, checking their handovers from one to another to make sure the overall presentation would be polished and well-paced. Sam was going to open briefly and introduce Sayeed, who would make his presentation and then hand over to Rosie, with Chris, Debbie and John following up. Jane had bagged last place, before Sam wrapped everything up.

They walked down to the meeting room together and Sam's hand was almost on the door handle when Debbie suddenly said: 'Sam, I'm really nervous! Suppose this all goes completely pear-shaped? I can't afford to lose this job.'

'I'm nervous too, Debbie,' said Chris suddenly, 'but I'm blowed if I am going to let that get in the way of saying what I really want to.

I know Arnold can be fierce but he really needs to hear this. We've all done a great job and he's not going to be sacking anyone.'

'Well said, Chris,' Sam chipped in. 'We have everything to be proud of and nothing to fear.'

'Except fear itself,' John added dryly.

'Come on,' said Jane. 'Eva gave us lots of good tips about dealing with nerves and her top one was be well prepared. And we know we've all done that, so let's get in there.'

'And get it over with,' said Debbie, adding quickly, 'I'll be all right. We'll all be all right.'

'We'll be better that that,' Sam said as he turned the door handle.

Nerves weren't helped by the sight of Dr Kramer already seated at the table. 'Come in,' he said in a tone that made it sound more like *'Come on!'* and they duly filed into the room and sat down, except Sam who made straight for the front of the room.

'A week may be a long time in politics, but a month is not very long to make major changes in a business,' Sam began when everyone had sat down and settled. Arnold Kramer frowned at that, and gave a slight shake of his head but Sam knew where he was going with this and didn't pause. 'As a team we have actually achieved an enormous amount in just four weeks, and more importantly we have laid the foundations of a great way forward. We are calling it BusinessPlus. It's a philosophy that as well as everyone doing their job well, everything we do adds something extra to the business. We think that's quite exciting and that's why I wanted the whole team here to talk about what they have done already and what's to come. Rosie is going to start off for us.'

'When Sam set me this challenge, I was, frankly, challenged. I couldn't see what I could do in a month to make DecisionMaker everyone's favourite place to be, even though I knew there was a lot more moaning than there used to be, and a lot of it about some very trivial things. Then Sam helped me hit on the idea of some quick wins. So I have sorted out the whole issue of locker space and bags being dumped around the place. To do that I had to go and negotiate with a number of different people and I realised that every time I heard one of these "bad" stories,' Rosie gestured with her first and second fingers on both hands to indicate the quote marks she was putting around 'bad', 'I felt a bit worse, a bit more down at heart. So then I decided that part of my role was to go around spreading all the good little stories. Every time I heard about something positive, I set about to spread that one around the business, and I found out two things. One, it wasn't difficult to do, and two, it was a very uplifting thing to do. I completed on a couple of other quick wins as well, which gave me some more good stories to tell. What I have noticed is that I have gained some allies, other people who like good news and positive stories as well. So our aim now is to make sure that the number of positive stories going around DecisionMaker is greater than the number of negative ones. I have done some research around this as well, and as a general rule, positive people work better, tend to be more collaborative, definitely don't blame other people so much and are more likely to go the extra mile to get something in on time or meet a deadline. All of which are the things we want to get back to at DecisionMaker.'

Arnold Kramer said nothing, but he looked interested and made a note in a small pocket notebook, which he slipped back into his pocket.

Sayeed was next. With a slick presentation he highlighted all the things in the old process that had contributed to the Monthly Cost Forecast being an exercise in putting together inaccurate data, and showed how he had focussed on creating a useful, detailed and informed report, with a commentary, highlights and a number of other features all adding insight and value to the business.

'So that's BusinessPlus on the Cost Forecast,' he explained. 'But what has really changed for me was that we had a conversation about accountability. And I realised I hadn't been taking ownership of the Cost Forecast. I had been treating it as something I was supposed to produce because that was my job. It hadn't occurred to me to make it something I could be really proud of, something that really added to the business, something where I could say: "Hey, that was mine – I did that!" So just like Rosie and the positive stories, I have been talking about accountability to everyone I have to get information from.'

'And how do they respond to that?' asked Dr Kramer with arched eyebrows.

'I have the same conversation Sam had with me,' Sayeed came back quickly. 'I ask them what's happening, how come, what can we do about that and who is going to do what.'

'I'll come back to that,' Kramer said, looking at Sayeed as the notebook came out again.

John stood up. A good contrast in style to Sayeed, John's more measured delivery and serious demeanour was calculated to keep Arnold Kramer's interest after an up-tempo start.

'Sam asked me to try to get to the bottom of what people are really thinking, especially in respect to what has changed. Of course we have our "Shout About It" staff survey, but that only really tells us what has changed in terms of the responses people give, year on year. So we applied some of the thinking we use to try and find out what our customers are thinking, to our own people. We wanted to look at three things: what people say they want, what they might actually want but haven't thought of, and what they think our purpose should be. It has had to be a very rapid dip sample in order to get any results at all back to you today, but what we have so far is very interesting.' As John revealed the results, together with a plan to widen the sample and analyse more data, Sam was quietly pleased to see Arnold Kramer nodding thoughtfully.

Chris started with a picture of a giant rat. 'Just joking,' she said, flicking quickly on to a slide showing the Rodent 1 Project. 'Well, we have been calling it the Risk Assessment Tool, or RAT for short. We recognise that it needs a better name, if only to avoid the acronym, but in the meantime we quite like those clever laboratory rats that find their way through mazes, so internally we are sticking with Rodent 1 for now. The plan here is to bring this forward very rapidly so that we have something new out there to shout about. The challenge had been that everyone thought this would jeopardise the MPE Project – that's all the work we are doing around Misleading Past Experiences in decision making. What we have been able to do is create a bit of a buzz around this – so much so that we now have a Rodent 1 Skunk Squad who have created a Sunday Club to work on new ideas. In fact, they have come up with one already – a diagnostic called the Team Decision Risk Indicator , or TDRI. The idea is to measure the appetite for risk of different individuals, so that teams can assess how they differ in that area and take their different attitudes to risk into account when making important decisions.

'Why don't I know about this?' asked Dr Kramer.

'Because the Skunk Squad only came up with it yesterday and asked me to tell you about it today. They'll be back to you early next week with a project specification, budgets, timelines and all of that.'

Arnold Kramer opened his mouth as if to say something but apparently thought better of it and nodded instead.

Debbie stepped up next. 'Sam told me to learn as much as I could about everything around the business, and other businesses, not just about the job I'm doing. So I set out to find out what all the parts of DecisionMaker really do.'

'Tell me,' said Arnold Kramer with a touch of irony.

'Well, one thing we do is go to an awful lot of meetings – which most people don't think add very much to what we are trying to do.'

'Interesting,' said Kramer, 'so...'

'So I looked at what some other businesses do. Everything from stand-up huddles, to having meeting protocols posted on the wall, to round-the-table formats. There are lots of ways we could ring the changes, and I have a few slides on that coming up.' Debbie went on, 'Sam also suggested I broaden my experience by looking for new responsibilities. Most importantly though, he told me to keep on asking for feedback, and above all to confront myself.'

'And have you? Confronted yourself, I mean,' asked Dr Kramer, looking half amused and half puzzled. 'I'm not sure I know what that means. Explain it to me.'

'Well, perhaps that is rather dramatic language,' Debbie admitted, 'but I know what he meant. It's about each of us being realistic about where we are, what we're good at and what we're not good at, and, well, being honest with ourselves instead of being the big "I am" all the time, which I now realise I was doing too much of the time.'

'And the effect of that?'

'Oh, I'm much happier and the team is much happier. Happiness isn't everything in business, but it beats unhappiness hands down,' responded Debbie, flicking on to a slide showing people drawing a large mind-map in a meeting, another group using coloured pens to draw images, a clock showing 11.48 a.m. as the starting time of a meeting, a meeting taking place on a basketball court, a table tennis bat with the words 'Move On!' written on it, and some other images.

'Interesting,' was Arnold Kramer's only comment when Debbie had run through a dozen different ways that DecisionMaker could make its meetings more energising, more creative and more productive. The notebook stayed in his pocket but he looked thoughtful again.

Then it was Jane's turn. 'I've learned to go past the bag drop on the way into a meeting – any meeting – to leave my baggage at the door and take my best self in,' she began. 'And not just meetings actually, but in everything I do. So I have been taking that around the organisation. I've gone from being a drain to a being a radiator! I'm talking about energy here. I realised I had become one of those people who drain all the energy out of a room rather than someone who radiates energy everywhere they go. Who wants to work with a drain,' she added, 'except possibly a plumber?'

'So what happened?' Jane asked suddenly, exactly as she had at the team meeting. 'What happened to change all that? To make me feel the way I used to about being here? To make me feel really positive?'

She certainly seemed to have Dr Kramer's attention.

'I got a brilliant manager!' she repeated. 'I got a manager who listened to me, who seemed to care about me and who seemed to be on my side.'

Sam had one slide to finish off with, summarising what had been achieved and what the team had planned for the next four weeks. He was still embarrassed by Jane's effusiveness and kept the closing part of the presentation crisp and to the point.

Arnold Kramer was leaning back in his chair. As Sam finished he sat forward and looked around the team. 'Thank you,' he said, 'thank you all.'

John began to stand up, saying, 'If there's nothing else?'

'Well, you have come up with considerably more than I was expecting. I am surprised – and you can take that in a positive way,' he added. 'Sam, I'd like a few minutes with you please.' Everyone else duly filed out of the room and Dr Kramer turned to Sam.

CHAPTER 26

TELL ME MORE

'Well, Sam,' Dr Kramer looked across the table, 'assuming you didn't just bribe them all, you seem to have done something remarkable to that team. What have you done?'

Anxious about just what Arnold Kramer would make of the team's presentations, Sam was caught out by the question. It took a moment before he realised that Arnold Kramer was smiling. Dr Kramer had leaned back in his chair, steepled his fingers and with eyes wide open and head cocked to one side was waiting, pleasantly, for Sam to reply.

'I have been giving that some thought myself,' Sam shook his head. 'I didn't have any training in how to be a manager, how to get the best out of other people. So the honest truth is, it was all a bit seat of the pants. What I realised very rapidly, though, is that it is all about the conversations you have with people.'

'Go on,' invited Kramer, looking genuinely interested.

'When I thought about it,' Sam continued, 'I realised that virtually all the conversations I've had, where I have been on what you might call the receiving end of a conversation with a manager, have been the same conversation. Usually about what I needed to do. More of, better, differently. Quite nicely delivered very often, but usually the same conversation. You've just seen six very different people. All in very different circumstances, with different motivations, at different stages in their careers and so on.' He glanced up. Arnold Kramer looked away for a moment then back at Sam.

'Rosie was mad keen but a bit all over the place. So we had a coaching conversation. Sayeed is great, but he hadn't really taken ownership of things, and a conversation about accountability needs to be quite different. John is a real old stager. Absolutely great. I was quite worried we might lose him but I managed something of a win-win there. I needed to give him something big and important to do, and show him that I trusted him to get on with it.'

'Delegation,' said Arnold Kramer, nodding. 'I was once told that is the crowning glory of leadership. You are making me think, Sam, that perhaps I haven't been doing enough of it.'

'Well, I wouldn't want to comment on that,' Sam said. 'Chris wanted a solid appraisal conversation, so that she knew what I was expecting and exactly where she stood. I know there are lots of organisations that have done away with the whole annual appraisal thing altogether but I think if it's done well it can contribute a lot. Debbie's was a career conversation. She is very ambitious – and capable of great things I think – but sort of expecting the business to do it for her.'

'What did you tell her?'

'Well you heard most of it from her,' Sam grinned, 'but we also talked about getting more exposure, finding a mentor, or a sponsor, expanding her networks and looking for opportunities. Not meaning finding another job,' he added quickly. 'It was a conversation intended to keep her on board, not send her into the arms of the competition!'

'And Jane?' asked Dr Kramer. 'You must have bribed *her*!' He was smiling but raised an eyebrow, looking for an answer from Sam.

'Well, it started off as a difficult conversation. You know, one where you have to tell someone something they don't want to hear. Jane was being...' he paused, 'well, let's just say she was being rather negative about things. To the point where I thought her behaviour wasn't acceptable. So I told her so. I did it in an orderly, structured way, and I think because of that, it did have a good effect. Because that was in the end a good conversation, or at the very least a necessary conversation, Jane came back to me about something else and I was able to help her.'

Kramer nodded again, adding: 'For which she seems extremely grateful.'

'I'm slightly embarrassed about that,' Sam admitted.

'Don't be.' Arnold Kramer stood up, walked the length of the table to the now blank projector screen then turned and came back. 'So you have had six conversations, one with each member of your team, but six very different conversations, and with that you have produced everything I've just seen up there,' he waved a hand at the screen.

'Well, I hadn't quite thought about it like that,' said Sam, 'but in a way, yes.'

'Well I want you to think about it like that, Sam. In fact, I want you to get everyone else in the company thinking like that. In fact, I am wondering whether you haven't started to do that already?'

Sam looked up, startled. 'No, I haven't really talked to anyone else about this. Well, I spoke to Gordon about something – he was very helpful actually – but that was him helping me.'

'I definitely thought I sensed a different atmosphere when I came in this morning,' Kramer said thoughtfully. 'There seemed to be a bit of a party atmosphere going on. Not that I want everyone partying, but...' He tailed off. Sam waited.

'I want you to spread what you have done right through the company, Sam,' he said, 'and I think you had better start with me. Perhaps I have more to learn than I thought about managing people. Tell me about these six conversations...'

CHAPTER 27

ONE MONTH LATER

Hoxton Square was busy. A hub of local entertainment and home to a host of bars, restaurants and clubs housed in the old Victorian buildings surrounding the central green with its plane trees, Sam found it a good place to slip out to for a few moments of fresh air and reflection from time to time. As he walked past the old White Cube Gallery building someone called his name. He turned to find his old boss, Kathy, smiling hesitantly at him.

'Sam, I thought that was you,' she said. 'Hello.'

'Hi Kathy, good to see you,' said Sam. 'How's things?'

'Well, if I'm honest,' said Kathy, 'not great.'

'What's the trouble?'

'I am not getting along at all with my new team. I just can't seem to get things across to them. To be honest it's been like herding cats, and I'm beginning to lose my rag with people. Which is not good and it's not helping.' Kathy took a sip of her drink. 'Heard great things about DecisionMaker though, sounds as though you're all on the up and up. How are you finding it?'

'To be frank,' Sam responded, 'I was out of my depth at first, but I had a couple of conversations and a bit of an eye-opening moment.'

'Which was? Don't keep me in suspense here!'

'Well, it started with Rosie. She seemed to be all over the place and I got her to focus on just a couple of things she could deliver and get those things done.'

'Well, you did better than me then. How did you do it?'

'As I discovered, but only after the event, and for the first time in my life, I held a coaching conversation.'

'And that was the eye-opener?'

'No, the eye-opener came a little while after that when I realised that a coaching conversation wouldn't solve all my problems.'

'Because?'

'Well, first of all because not every situation is a coaching situation.' Kathy nodded and Sam went on. 'But much more importantly, it was the realisation that I had never thought about different types of conversation before.'

'Go on,' said Kathy, 'you're beginning to interest me.'

'I realised that I just used to have one conversation. Didn't matter what the situation was, I was holding pretty much the same conversation with everyone all the time. You know, the one about what we need to do, what the objectives are, what the numbers are and so on.'

'Oh,' said Kathy. 'Oh dear.'

'Are you OK?'

'Yes. I think I may be having an eye-opening moment, that's all.' Kathy paused then went on. 'So where did you find out about all these different types of conversation?'

'Well,' said Sam, 'there's a bit of a story attached to that. Have you got a few minutes?'

PART II: THE CONVERSATIONS

The idea for *The Six Conversations of a Brilliant Manager* had been with me for a long time before I finally sat down to write it. That's partly because a busy schedule running a successful consulting business, coaching individuals and delivering workshops meant that my priority was often elsewhere. It is also because it was only in the course of doing all those other things that the concept crystallised over time. Working with leaders and managers from all walks of life, I came to realise that what makes some people more successful than others is the *quality of the conversations* they have with others. It took me a lot longer to work out that these high performers know that they need to take a different approach to different conversations – and that the simplest way to do that is to have *a different structure for each conversation*.

If you have enjoyed reading about how Sam Mitchell learned to use the Six Conversations of a Brilliant Manager and want a simple reference guide to each of them – or if you just want to cut to the chase of exactly what the six different conversations are – then Part II is for you.

Conversation #1: 'What can you do about that?'

The essence of this conversation is to work through the four-part structure *only asking questions*. As soon as you start 'telling', offering advice or making suggestions, you have stopped coaching. That's because coaching works firstly by raising the other person's awareness of things, and then by getting them to take responsibility – for setting their own goals through to working out how they will achieve them. If you tell someone what you think, you deny their awareness; if you tell them what to do, you take away their responsibility.

Here is the structure of **Conversation #1: 'What can you do about that?'**

1. Help the person to identify a good goal.
2. Help them to work out where they are in respect to the goal – where they are starting from.
3. Help them to identify some options – different ways to achieve the goal, or different ways to get started; don't just go with the first idea.
4. Make sure they tell you what they are going to do, what their first action will be, when they will do it and when they will come back to tell you that they have done it!

The coaching approach is to be non-judgemental and to use collaborative language so that **Conversation #1: 'What can you do about that?'** is based in equality, builds commitment and creates change together.

Conversation #2: 'Who should really own this?'

This is a very different conversation, although it too has a four-part structure. Your first intention here should be to find out what the situation actually is, getting down to hard facts. Then it's about finding out how the situation has occurred. The critical thing here is to avoid blame. **Conversation #2: 'Who should really own this?'** is based around four questions:

1. Where are we now?
2. How did we get here?
3. What can we do?
4. Who's doing what – and by when?

The purpose of 'Where are we now?' is to get to the facts of the matter. That doesn't mean not talking about feelings – the fact of the matter may be that someone's feelings have been badly hurt – but 'The facts, just the facts,' is a useful motto to keep things on track here.

The idea behind the 'How did we get here?' stage is to find out exactly how the current situation arose, particularly if it is one you don't want to happen again. The crucial thing here is to avoid falling into the trap of blame, or sounding as if you are blaming someone. As Sam points out to Sayeed, no-one gets up in the morning and goes into work hoping to be blamed for something, so blame is never productive. In 'How did we get here?' your aim should be to find out just enough to prevent the same situation recurring. Think of it like adjusting a piece of machinery. The machine was producing what you wanted. Now it has produced something that is not right. You need to go to the control panel, see what has changed or gone out of adjustment and modify the settings accordingly. Blaming the machine won't get you very far.

'What can we do?' promotes a collaborative problem-solving approach. Two heads are better than one, so solve the problem, or find a good way forward, together. Remember though that this is a conversation to promote accountability, so ideally you want the other person to come up with a solution. They will certainly need to 'own' it. Which leads neatly on to part four of **Conversation #2: 'Who should really own this?'**

'Who's doing what, and by when?' is vital. The problem with collaborative solutions is that they are very easily stated in terms of

'What we need to do.' And the problem with that is that most things are not things 'we' can do. So each person has to be explicit about what they are going to do – and when. It is a good rule to sum up this conversation by saying out loud what both parties have agreed to, or even better, you say exactly what you are going to do and have the other person tell you exactly what they are committing to doing.

Conversation #3: 'How should we be behaving?'

'Difficult' conversations come in many guises. Usually they are difficult because we think the other person is going to react badly. After all, if you think the other person is going to agree enthusiastically with everything you want to say, you are unlikely to approach the conversation thinking it will be difficult!

That bad reaction we are anticipating might be resistance to the message, taking offence or becoming upset or angry. Or it may be that you don't relish confrontation, feel you are letting someone down – or that they will challenge you, or resent you afterwards. None of which is very helpful.

So the first thing to do is try to frame the conversation more positively to yourself. Instead of 'giving some tough feedback' you could think of 'having a highly developmental conversation'. Instead of telling someone this is their last chance, you could think of helping them save their job. Sam's conversation with Jane is really about a change in behaviour. Although there are other 'difficult' conversations, for example telling someone something won't be delivered on time, or telling someone that their job has been made redundant, this structure is focussed on the conversation where you need someone to stop doing something, start doing something, or do something differently. It goes like this:

1. State the problem behaviour.
2. Say why it is a problem.
3. Say what you expect.
4. Ask for their perspective.
5. Ask for their solution(s).
6. If you can accept their solution, do. If not, say what solution you can accept.
7. Summarise the solution and agree when you will review it.

By defining the problem behaviour and saying why it is a problem, you take charge of the conversation. The 'why' might be the impact it has on other people, that it is contrary to the organisation's values, or any number of things, but make sure you can provide sustainable evidence. If your 'why' is simply 'it annoys/upsets me' perhaps you should look in the mirror for a few moments before holding this particular conversation! Saying what you expect sets the standard.

It is steps 4 and 5 which are most important though. You do not have to accept the other person's solution. If it is completely unacceptable, and you cannot come up with something better between the two of you, then you may have to impose your solution, but that is always the least effective way. As with **Conversation #2: 'Who should really own this?'** given the chance, most people will suggest something which improves the situation.

Finally, state very clearly what the rules are going forward, whether it is their solution, your solution or one arrived at together, and be clear that you will both meet and review things after a period of time.

Conversation #4: 'Who's really doing this?'

This conversation can really set you free, and learning it can change your life!

Whilst delegation can be a source of difficulties, many more problems are caused by managers who don't or won't delegate. For some people non-delegation is practically an addictive behaviour, and many organisations are systematically under-delegated, with everyone doing tasks they really should have briefed others to do.

You may be unable or unwilling to let go, lack faith in other abilities, or lack the self-confidence to delegate properly. If you find yourself saying things like: *'It's quicker to do it myself,'* and *'If you want something done properly, do it yourself,'* then look out! What all these things usually conceal is the need to feel indispensable, and the sneaking suspicion that a well-delegated manager will have nothing left to do and be an obvious candidate for redundancy or downsizing. If your mindset is 'only I can do this,' or 'no-one does this as well as me (because I *am* a superior being),' then you will never learn to delegate.

In this conversation you need to set the scene. Give the other person the reason *why* you want it done and why you are asking them to do it. Be clear about *what* needs doing, and *when* it has to be done by. Talk through *who* else might be involved. In Sam's conversation with John, *where* it will be done is not relevant, but it might be to you. In which case you will need to cover that off as well. Note that Sam does **not** talk about *how* John is going to get it done, and neither should you. That's up to the person you are delegating to. So **Conversation #4: 'Who's really doing this?'** looks like this:

1. Set the scene.
2. Describe the task.
3. Set the timeline.
4. Be clear on the limits of authority.
5. Check the other person's understanding of the four key points.

In a more complex situation you may need to cover phases of delivery, or intermediate milestones, what resources are or can be made available, and administrative issues or issues around working with other departments.

The most important thing to remember is that anything you delegate will not be done exactly the way you would have done it. Think about writing a report as an example. No two people have exactly the same writing style so no matter how tight the guidelines, a report will always, to some extent, reflect the writing style of the author. We are not talking about a different quality standard – just doing it differently. That's why Sam does not tell John *how* to do it.

Conversation #5: 'Where are we heading?'

The key to this conversation is that you are *not* taking on responsibility for the other person's career – that's their responsibility. You can be a brilliant manager, however, by helping them and guiding their thinking around their career. Listening to hundreds of managers talking about career conversations shows that this is the crucial distinction. Once you stop thinking that you are in some way being held responsible for the other person's progress or lack of it, it becomes a different and much more useful conversation. Of course, if part of your management role is to nominate people for 'Talent Programmes' or other fast-track approaches then you do have some responsibility, at least in the short term, but this career conversation will still supply you with a sound structure for explaining your decisions.

The key points you need to get across to the other person are that they need to:

1. Fortify themselves with knowledge.

2. Broaden their experience and raise their profile as much as possible.
3. Look for new responsibilities.
4. Ask for feedback.
5. Confront themselves – work out what they really are good at, accept that we all have limitations, be honest with themselves about what they really want, and hear what other people say.

Huge changes have taken place in organisations in recent years. Typically organisations have become much 'flatter' with fewer layers of hierarchy between the most junior and most senior people. Many organisations are working to eliminate concepts like 'junior' and 'senior' altogether. All of which can lead people to wonder what a career looks like in the modern world. In my consulting business, requests to train managers to hold good career conversations have been on the increase for some time. Sam's conversation with Chris is a distillation of those training sessions.

The more traditional assumptions a lot of people still hold are that:

- Most people follow a straight line career path to retirement.
- Career development means upward mobility.
- Only new or young employees can be developed.
- Career development relates primarily to work experience.

A more realistic set of assumptions are that:

- Career paths are increasingly diverted and interrupted.
- Career development can be facilitated by lateral and even downward moves.
- Learning and change can occur at any age and career stage.

- Career development is influenced by family, personal and community roles, and can be facilitated by work outside paid employment.

Conversation #5: 'Where are we heading?' is all about helping the other person to see the wood for the trees and to take responsibility for their own career. Master this one and you will soon have a great reputation as a business mentor.

Conversation #6: 'How are we doing?'

The dreaded appraisal! Loathed and feared in almost equal proportions, by almost everyone taking part. But it doesn't have to be that way. You can hold a really high quality appraisal conversation by using the following structure. Sam's conversation with Chris follows a very specific form, designed on sound psychological principles to avoid most of the traps and pitfalls that plague so many appraisal meetings. It works like this:

1. Recognise - recent achievements.
2. Empathise - 'listen and learn'.
3. Encourage - what do they want to improve?
4. Ask - them to consider your suggestions.
5. Coach - using **Conversation #1: The Coaching Conversation**.
6. Build - their confidence in future success!

Although you very definitely want to hear things from the other person's point of view, simply asking: 'So, how do *you* think it's gone?' or something similar, is not usually a very good way to begin. That's because it is important that you take charge of the conversation right at the beginning, not simply hand it over to the other person to start off by listing all their achievements and triumphs. You do of course want to listen carefully to what they have to say, but that comes in a minute. Here are the details of the six parts of **Conversation #6: 'How are we doing?'**

Part 1 - Recognise

Recognise simply means find something they have been doing well, or at the very least acceptably, and tell them what it is. No need to list everything; in fact, don't do that at this stage. Recognise something that has been going well, and then say that you would like to get their view, or understand their own perspective on their performance and how they have done against their objectives.

Part 2 - Empathise

Now you need to **Empathise** – that is to understand what the other person truly thinks, feels and believes. That's a slightly broader definition than most dictionaries give, but the 'think' and 'believe' parts are every bit as important as the 'feel'. In fact, the behaviour I am proposing here is that you ask good open questions designed to get the other person talking, that you listen without interruption and without making judgments (which is harder), and that you take good notes. Then, when the other person has told you everything they want to, you sum up to them what they have just told you.

This has a quite extraordinary effect. It shows you have given the other person the gift of seeking to truly understand their point of view, their perspective on things. You have genuinely seen it their way before telling them you disagree, hold a different opinion, see it slightly differently, or anything of that sort. It is actually quite rare in life for any of us to think that someone else really understands where we are coming from, and it is a very precious feeling. So if you do this well, you bring into play what psychologists call *reciprocity*. This principle has been observed all over the world and in every type of culture from the most sophisticated to the most primitive. In its simplest form it says that if I do something for you, you will feel that you should do something for me. That's not to say that you always *will* do something, but the feeling of obligation seems to be almost universal.

Part 3 - Encourage

In my experience, and that of many other managers who have adopted this approach, if you really do listen, without commenting, and then feed back exactly what you have heard, the other person is more than likely to move, with the smallest of nudges, to talking about things that have not gone so well, areas for improvement and so on. This is the **Encourage** part of this conversation. In the book Sam simply asks Chris: 'So, is there anything you think you could have done better, or should improve going forwards?'

Part 4 - Ask

That is not to say that the other person will come forward with everything you as a manager might be looking for at this point, but if you have done the first part really well then you should still have a little bit of reciprocity left in the tank when you **Ask**. So this is the point where Sam adds in what he wants Chris to do, that she has not mentioned yet.

The aim is that at this point of the conversation you have agreement about what is going to happen going forward: new objectives, skills, capabilities or behavioural development – whatever it might be – and you are talking to someone who is willing. That's because you listened, showed that you had understood, and asked them for their thoughts and ideas before chipping in with your own.

Part 5 - Coach

As we already know from **Conversation #1: 'What can you do about that?'** with Rosie, a willing person can be coached. So at this point you use your coaching skills and the structure of **Conversation #1: 'What can you do about that?'** to get to clear actions, timelines and agreements.

Part 6 - Build Confidence

Finally, to end this conversation, do not go back into praise! It is an easy trap to fall into. The *Recency* effect tells us that we tend to remember the last part of a conversation best. The *Primacy* effect tells us that we are likely to remember the beginning better than the middle. So we remember the beginning and the end of a conversation best. For this conversation to be at its most powerful it should end with a future-focus, not a look back into the past. So instead of praising what has been done, finish by **Building Confidence**. Build the other person's confidence that they can do everything they have agreed, that they are capable of performing well and perhaps even of exceeding expectations – their own as well as yours!

And finally

While I was still busy writing this second part of *The Six Conversations of a Brilliant Manager* someone asked me, 'But what about the pay rise conversation? The one where someone comes in, explains all the great stuff they have been doing and pitches you for a pay rise that you can't give them?'

That's the point at which you have to decide *which conversation* to have. It might be **Conversation #1: 'What can you do about that?'** it might be **Conversation #5: 'Where are we heading?'** or if they come with a belligerent or aggressive attitude, it could even be **Conversation #3: 'How should we be behaving?'**

The point is that you decide. You make a judgement on which conversation is going to get the best result for both of you, and then you use the appropriate structure to keep that conversation on track. That stops things veering off in an unexpected direction, and it stops you reducing everything to 'these are the numbers and what we need to do is…'!

ACKNOWLEDGEMENTS

My deep and heartfelt thanks go first and foremost to Heather Codling, who has been the inspirational mainspring and life force of Vybrant for the past decade and nagged me to write this book for a long time until I finally did it. Heather is very closely followed by Vybrant co-founder Julie Goodwin and colleagues Julia Tildesley, Bernadette Rogers and Juliet Courtney. The list of Vybrant associates who have contributed energy, ideas, creative thinking and brilliant suggestions would be too long to name here but I do want to single out Anthony Sheldon, Russell Houghton and Jonathan Cook for their ongoing support, friendship and coaching, as well as for their insight and willingness to share their experience. Jacq Burns, co-founder of the London Writers' Club, contributed greatly to the overall concept, especially in the early days, and continues to be a source of inspiration and motivation; Abi Layton made sure the finished product was actually finished. And of course my wife and co-conspirator Pam, who knows when to ask how it is going, and when not to.

For constant inspiration, support and professional guidance, enormous thanks to Carrie Bedingfield and the team at Onefish Twofish, and of course to Clare Christian, Julia Pidduck, and all the team at RedDoor for having faith in the idea of *The Six Conversations* and for bringing it into being.

A huge thank you goes to Todd Cherches for editing the US edition of *The Six Conversations*. Todd is the CEO and co-founder of BigBlueGumball, an innovative New York City-based leadership consulting, training, and executive coaching firm. He is also a top-rated, two-time award-winning Adjunct Professor of Leadership at the NYU School of Professional Studies, in the Division of Programs in Business, as well as a lecturer on leadership at Columbia University. Todd is currently engaged in writing his first book: *VisuaLeadership®: Leveraging the Power of Visual Thinking in Leadership and in Life*, to be published in 2020 by Post Hill Press/Simon & Schuster.

Especially though I want to thank our Vybrant clients. All the CEOs and other leaders, including head teachers, who have agreed to be interviewed, all the teams it has been so motivational to work with, and most of all the thousands of workshop participants who have responded so enthusiastically to the concept of structured conversations and whose input, feedback and enthusiasm have contributed directly to Sam Mitchell's story.

The four fixations of a brilliant leader

Alan J. Sears

"The Four Fixations of a Brilliant Leader is quite simply a brilliant book."
Carrie Bedingfield

THE FOUR FIXATIONS OF A BRILLIANT LEADER

CHAPTER 1

A week may be a long time in politics but sometimes it can feel even longer in business. It had been a tough week for Julie-Anne Johnson and it was only Thursday. She was tired and she knew it. Her boss in the USA, Ted, was a good man and a good boss, but he would work on American time, so his day started halfway through Julie-Anne's and his afternoon was her evening. She didn't like to complain, but Wednesday had ended with another long transatlantic phone call that had finished at 11 p.m. She had been in her office until seven o'clock, got home at eight o'clock, having missed the children's bedtime, and started early on Thursday morning to drive to Bristol.

She could have asked Albert to come to her office, at the opposite end of the M4, but she knew that he would want to bring in members of his team to explain their own thinking and ideas. It was a way of giving them credit. Albert also liked to bring people in at no notice for impromptu creativity sessions. All told, if she was going to access the best that Albert's agency had to offer then she would be better off taking the long haul. As it turned out, the day had gone well, at least until she hit the evening traffic coming out of Reading on the way back. By the time she had made it back to her home near Windsor the children were tucked up in bed, bedtime stories read and lights out.

'Tomorrow,' she told her husband Ed, 'I am working in my own office, I *am* going to leave in good time, come hell or high water, and I am going to be back for bath and bedtime before my children forget who I am!'

The call came at 10 p.m. Julie-Anne rolled her eyes, put down her glass of wine and picked up her mobile. It would be 5 p.m. in Philadelphia. As always though, Ted Williams was apologetic.

'Hi Julie-Anne,' he began, 'I know it's late with you, and I'm sorry, but this is something of an emergency.' Bad figures? Bad press? A product recall? Julie-Anne rapidly ticked off the possibilities, but was still caught out when Ted said: 'It's Rex, Rex Tollman, he's had a heart attack.'

Julie-Anne knew Rex, liked him and respected him as a colleague. Rex ran the Imaging business of XYZ Healthcare. It manufactured and distributed a very successful product used, ironically enough, in the detection of heart disease. It was a small division in Europe, and most of the people in it had worked together for a long time. Although it was part of the larger global division, it still had the air of a family business about it, a helpful, collaborative culture where people got on well together. The news about Rex would be a shock to them.

'How is he?' Julie-Anne asked straight away. 'Is there any news?'

'He's been taken to hospital, and that's really all I know at the moment. His wife called John Harris and let him know, and John called me.' John was the Marketing Director for the Division and not someone Julie-Anne knew well. There was a pause until Julie-Anne filled it, asking: 'So…?'

'I want you to step into Rex's shoes, at least for the time being.'

'But what about John Harris, or the rest of the leadership team over there? Surely any one of them is better placed than me to take over until Rex is back. I don't know the business at all.'

'I know that, Julie-Anne, but I think you have just the qualities the business needs right now, and I'm not sure that applies to any of the rest of that team just at present.'

'Well, I'm not sure just how kindly they would take to someone coming in from outside. What exactly is it you think I've got that they need so badly?'

At other end Ted paused, took a breath and then carried on.

ABOUT THE AUTHOR

ALAN SEARS is Head Honcho at Vybrant Organisation Ltd, a consultancy specialising in leadership, management and top team development. He has worked with thousands of leaders and managers, from FTSE 100 companies to SMEs and start-ups, the public sector and not-for-profit organisations.

alanjsears.com
alanjsears.com/six-conversations-brilliant-manager-book/

@alanjsears
Linkedin: Alan J Sears (linkedin.com/in/alsears/)

To find out more about Alan Sears, or sign up for email
updates about new books, visit

alanjsears.com

You can get in touch with Alan via:

@alanjsears

Alan J Sears

Find out more about RedDoor Press and sign up
to our newsletter to hear about our latest releases,
author events, blog tours, exciting competitions,
cover reveals and book trailers at

reddoorpress.co.uk

YOU CAN ALSO FOLLOW US:

@RedDoorBooks

Facebook.com/RedDoorPress

@reddoorbooks

Red Door